THE RYDER CUP '85

THE RYDER CUP '85

Introduction by TONY JACKLIN

Pelham Books
LONDON

First published in Great Britain by
Pelham Books Ltd
44 Bedford Square
London WC1B 3DP
1985

The Ryder Cup '85
  1 Ryder Cup – History
  I Jacklin, Tony
  796.352′74′0941   GV970

ISBN 0-7207-1678-0

Designed, edited and produced by First Editions
319 City Road, London EC1V 1LJ

Executive editor: David Emery

Typeset by Presentia Art, Horsham
Origination by Trend Add
Printed by W.S. Cowell Ltd, Ipswich

Contents

Tony Jacklin

Introduction
by Tony Jacklin

When the time comes to sit back and reflect there is little doubt I shall be hard pressed to decide which of four major triumphs gave me the most personal satisfaction.

Today I suppose I would put winning The British Open in 1969 first, captaining the European team to victory in the Ryder Cup a very close second, winning the US Open and my first venture as Ryder Cup captain in 1983, equal third.

It is not easy to separate what were great and incredible peaks because golf is basically a selfish game, thankfully played by mostly generous people.

Winning the 1969 Open was a great personal triumph but one which I think the nation shared with me. As a player it is the title everyone dreams about. To achieve it is the supreme accolade to personal skill. There is no greater honour.

The Ryder Cup is different. It is a victory to be shared and relished by everyone. You can travel Europe saying "I won The Open" and the response comes back "We won the Ryder Cup."

That is the real joy, for at the end of the day the game is where it belongs. With the people. They relate to triumph and, my goodness, didn't we hear it from those awesome galleries at The Belfry.

Without belittling in any way the US Open, I have to admit that winning that prestigious title 11 months after the Royal Lytham Open was really a personal issue between me and the

The victorious American Ryder Cup team, Florida 1983

American players. I wanted to show them that I was an equal, worth my place in their top division and when I proved it by seven shots I was mentally telling them "Get hold of that." I had made my point, emphatically, and it gave me tremendous personal satisfaction.

The new realms are the Ryder Cup. Here, rather like the trainer of a heavyweight boxing champion, you can only pray that you have got the preparation right because once the bell goes it is all down to the fighter.

That is why I will always regard Florida, 1983, when Europe lost by a single point, as a magnificent effort by 12 splendid fighters. The only thing we did wrong over there was to lose $14\frac{1}{2}$-$13\frac{1}{2}$, but in my personal memory bank that performance remains a great triumph and proved to be the harbinger of the things to come at The Belfry.

Strangely, and it struck me most forcibly during our final practice rounds, it seemed as if there had been no time lapse at all between Florida, 1983 and The Belfry, 1985. It was as though we were starting the second round of a major championship having just shot 66 in the first.

Perhaps it was because I began worrying about it 18 months earlier; in fact, from the moment I was reappointed captain. From then on I was watching closely the results of every tournament carrying qualifying points for the team; checking the form of the players as the team gradually emerged.

From my own experience as a player in seven Ryder Cup teams I was determined to weld a togetherness – both on and off the course – that was not always apparent in my playing days. I didn't want players drifting off on their separate ways at six o'clock with just "See you in the morning", as the final goodnight message.

So for eight months I worked with Brian Cash, chief executive at The Belfry, setting up an atmosphere which guaranteed we had rooms to eat together, relax together and although we had waitress service we had complete privacy and an almost family intimacy.

I am very much a family man myself and would never have achieved the successes I have had without the support of my wife, Viv, so the first edict to the team was "Wives are most welcome." I am certain their presence at The Belfry was a big factor in the "togetherness" ideal I wanted.

It seemed, coming into the final practice round, we had got things pretty right. Morale was high. The players were in that perfect frame of mind – keyed up for the off, yet relaxed.

Still, there was a strange apprehension, bred, I suppose from the real knowledge that golf is a very fickle game and fanned by the enormous pressure that had been put on the team by the insistence of the media that this time we would win.

We had, after all, The Open champion, Sandy Lyle, the US Masters champion, Bernhard Langer and the inimitable Severiano Ballesteros, past winner of both (and so soon afterwards to underline his incredible talents by winning the World Match Play championship for a fourth time) spearheading the team. The media optimism and the mood of expectancy from the galleries was understandable.

Yet having suffered the disappointment of defeat by a single point two years earlier, the thought of failure again – always a strong possibility in golf – was unbearable.

So I tried to make the pre-match build up as low key as possible. I wanted a confident team but not cocky overconfidence and the first reminder to me, personally, came during the final practice round.

It had been my intention to pair Ballesteros with Jose Rivero but after 13 holes I could see it was not working. I do not know if playing with Sevvy undermined Rivero's confidence a little . . . if

The Captain with Ballesteros and Pinero at The Belfry

he was in awe of him, or what. All I knew was that the pairing was not working so I pulled Manuel Pinero out of his partnership with Canizares in the match behind and put him in with Sevvy for the last four holes.

That pairing produced three out of a possible four points over the first two days of foursomes and fourballs.

My decision to pair Langer with Nick Faldo was based absolutely on the marvellous job they did for us together in Florida two years earlier. I saw no reason why it should not work again. In the event it didn't so I had to break that up and Langer went on to partner Canizares, then Lyle and finally Ken Brown to produce two more points from a possible four.

Langer was marvellous, so strong; I felt he would always give us a chance, partnering anyone.

I rested Lyle from the Saturday foursomes only because I felt that – like many of us – he doesn't really enjoy that form of golf, but it seemed the real stunner was my decision to rest Sam Torrance and Howard Clark from the Saturday afternoon foursomes even though they had beaten Tom Kite and Andy North in the morning fourballs.

The reason for that was simple. It would have been totally unfair to leave any player to make his debut in the Sunday singles.

It felt good once victory was achieved

The atmosphere on the course was mind-boggling, the tension unbelievable. Rivero had to come in with Canizares, a partnership that had, anyway, won the World Cup for Spain. The record shows they beat Kite and Calvin Peete seven and five, which is about as conclusive a margin as you can get.

Lunch on Friday was not exactly an hilarious affair with a score reading Europe one United States three, but I didn't come the heavy stuff. There were no pep talks, no recriminations. We just had a frank discussion about the way every player was feeling inside himself.

What emerged was that a few of the players – and I agree with them totally – are not too fond of foursomes golf. It is hard to do yourself justice when you are hitting someone else's ball, but in the afternoon fourballs we closed the gap to just a single point. All the pre-match euphoria had blown away. There was hard work to be done and the team did it on the second day to take us into the final singles with the two point lead I had hoped for.

The singles, which we won seven and a half to three and a half marked the day European golf came of age. I shall remember, for as long as I live, the birdie putt Sam Torrance holed on the last green to clinch the European victory but until he holed it I was as nervous and as uptight as I had been all week.

But when that putt dropped all the pent up emotions were released. A lot of the players wept their joy. We embraced. We celebrated. Some of us very near drowned.

For a week I hadn't slept very well, hadn't eaten much and lost six pounds in weight. If there is any credit to me for this momentus win then it was given me by the players. They did the job. They were my inspiration.

Let no-one suggest the victory was secured because American golf is in a bit of a decline. Our win was achieved by 12 players who gave 110 per cent and among them we can honestly claim to have two, if not three, who are the best in the world.

Between them they have given the game back to the millions who love it and I am sure there will be rich dividends to come . . . from Spain, from Italy, from Germany, from France, and, I wouldn't be surprised, from Sweden.

In golfing terms, Europe is on the boil thanks to that Ryder Cup win.

I am proud of a great, great team.

1 *Jacklin's Triumph*
by John Morgan

We waited a long time for the coming of Tony Jacklin. For close on 20 years golf had produced British winners, gutsy performers like Rees and Faulkner, Alliss and Thomas, Brown and Huggett but no-one with the charisma of that great champion and three times winner of The Open, Henry Cotton.

He was, and still is, The Maestro, a giant as a player and by his own life style – champagne, caviar and Bentleys – raised the status of the golf professional to a level whereby they no longer sneaked into clubhouses through the tradesmen's entrance but strode proudly through every red-carpeted portal as artists rather than artisans.

So great was the influence of The Maestro that after his epic round of 65 on his way to winning the 1934 Open at Sandwich, Dunlop dedicated a golf ball to him. Half a century later the Dunlop 65 is still a best seller.

Then came Jacklin. He marked his arrival in 1963 as winner of Henry Cotton's Rookie of the Year award and what he saw when he came to Cotton's palatial London home to collect his £100 prize convinced him that golf would give him a far better life style than his seeming destiny – a steel worker in his home town Scunthorpe.

Bill Shankland, the club professional at Potters Bar, who gave Jacklin his start as his assistant, had earlier impressed that very point, always adding there were no short cuts to riches. It could only be work, work and more work. So, under Shankland's steely eye, Jacklin worked. And how it paid!

In 1967 he won the Dunlop Masters at Royal St George's and – was this to be an omen? – holed in one, a TV transmitted spectacular that was to set the tongues wagging and the pulses racing. Now he was "Jacko", two years later to become "Our Jacko" as the nation claimed him following his Open championship win at Lytham.

He was the first British winner since Max Faulkner a long 28 years earlier. For the next four years he strode the fairways chirpily, cockily, inspired by such an incredible talent that was to win him 25 titles in 13 countries around the world.

In the process he sold the game of golf to the nation in a fashion Saatchi and Saatchi would have envied. Sandy Lyle, coincidentally to become the next Briton to win golf's greatest prize 16 years later and Nick Faldo, to name but two of Europe's triumphant Ryder Cup team, were seduced along with thousands of other youngsters by the exploits of Jacko, rapturously followed on TV and through the newspapers, to become addicts to the game.

But then, sadly, as Jacko himself would say "The wheels came off." The breakdown, I will always maintain, began at the Muirfield Open in 1972. There may have been many other contributory factors but it was, in the words of American golfer, Dave Marr, "The week God was a Mexican", that marked the beginning of the decline. The Mexican was, of course, Lee Trevino. But more of that later.

Ryder Cup action began for Jacko at Houston, Texas, in 1967, the first of seven consecutive appearances in the team and even today his contribution of 17 points from 35 matches (13 wins, eight halves) remains the highest by any British or European player. Peter Oosterhuis (28 matches), Bernard Gallacher (31) and Neil Coles (40) share second place with $15\frac{1}{2}$ points each. Peter Alliss, now the famed voice of TV golf, subscribed 15 points from 30 matches between 1953 and 1969.

But 1969 was the year. First, The Open victory at Lytham. Then the famous halved Ryder Cup match at Birkdale.

Jacko, who was never beaten in any match and contributed five out of a possible six points, had thrashed the mighty Jack Nicklaus four and three in the morning singles on the final day. They were paired again in the afternoon, last match out. Jacko, one down standing on the 17th, holed a monster eagle putt right across the green to square the match coming to the final hole and to again provide TV with another magical moment. Who will ever

Tony Jacklin with the Open Championship Trophy 1969

forget the picture of Jacko's caddie, heavy golf bag over his shoulder, leaping high into the air to punch his delight into an atmosphere leadened by the ecstatic cheers from the huge galleries?

Or that moment, some 20 minutes later, when Nicklaus, having run his ball a good four feet past the cup, holed one of the greatest pressure putts of all time and then picked up Jacko's ball, a still missable two feet away and handed it to Tony saying: "You wouldn't have missed that."

It was a wonderful act of sportsmanship – even though the American team were not totally unanimous in their approval – which made an indelible impression on Jacko. He says "It was a player to player gesture." But it was more. It was a mark of respect.

It was the then world's greatest golfer telling one of his closest challengers to that title that he was not going to allow the possibility of the Ryder Cup being won and lost because someone three putted the final green. Not after such an epic match.

Out of that euphoria strode Jacko to even more. He searched round the world . . . Australia, Japan, South America, Europe and, of course, stormed the citadel itself . . . America.

Eleven months after his Open win at Lytham he was wearing the crown of US Open champion, first British golfer to capture that coveted jewel since Ted Ray, way back in 1920. There were more notches on the victory belt. Twice he won the Jacksonville Open to leave hardened US golf writers wincing: "If he does it once more we'll make 'em rename it the Tony Jacklin Benefit."

He was set to destroy St Andrews at the 1970 Open when, after a fog-delayed start he covered the first nine holes in an audacious 29 strokes. In the press centre we were betting on a first round 60, perhaps better. But, as though the Gods were outraged at the cheek of the young man, a storm broke, play was suspended and, resuming next morning in totally changed conditions, Jacko shot a highly commendable 67. Had he got the 60 no-one would have caught him. As it was he finished fifth.

The following year at Royal Birkdale he was third behind the man who was to loom ever larger in his life, Lee Trevino.

As sports editor of the Daily Express I had signed up Jacklin to write about his many exploits around the world and by 1972 he was a fairly regular contributor to the newspaper. The obvious pressures of The Open championship required that I depute someone to be by his side, as it were, and available at the end of each round to summarise Tony's reactions to his own performance and record his innermost thoughts as the championship progressed. After Jacklin's approval the words duly appeared in the next morning's Daily Express.

16

After not too lengthy deliberations I deputed myself (as I had, regularly, in the past) and from this highly privileged position inside the roped fairways I followed at close range every piece of the dramatic action. To this day those final two rounds by Jacklin and Trevino remain the most absorbing, the most spectacular and the most thrilling I have ever seen from two players on any golf course anywhere in the world.

For although there was more than a substance of truth in the David Marr assertion that this was the week God was to become a Mexican Trevino, certainly blessed with every stroke of good fortune, played exquisitely and often, audaciously.

On one occasion he played a long par four hole back to front, hitting a five iron off the tee and then driving a wood into the heart of the green. The ploy: to enable him to play his second shot before Jacklin, gamble on getting it close and thus intensify the pressure on Tony as he stood over his second shot. Such was Trevino's supreme shot-making skill that he was able to set himself these sort of challenges which few other players would contemplate.

Had Jacklin played badly the final bitterness of defeat would have been more bearable. But he didn't. He played brilliantly.

He withstood a six-birdie Trevino barrage over the closing holes of the third round, replying with four of his own and from tee to green over those two enthralling days was, technically anyway, the better player.

What he could not legislate for was that moment when Trevino, bunkered on a short hole and with a difficult hanging lie, thinned the ball out at such an alarming speed that had it not hit the flagstick plumb centre it would surely have finished 25 yards over the back of the green in unplayable rough.

Instead, defying all logical ballistical law, the ball dropped straight into the hole – a million to one against birdie.

In the quiet sanctity of his rented house later that evening Jacklin, grey-faced and mentally drained, told me: "If I thought I had to go through that every day of my life, I would shoot myself now."

Next day, standing on the final tee, he must almost have wished he had for, at the preceding hole, the wheels had really come off.

Golf writers Keith MacKie and Ben Wright (now a successful TV commentator in the United States) stood with me by that ill-fated 17th tee as Jacklin looked set to claim his second Open title. His drive, long and accurately placed in the right side of the fairway, was in position A. Trevino drove into a bunker and his precise

At Muirfield in 1972 during the ill-fated final round against Trevino

reaction to that was: "Aw, s--t . . . that's blown it." At that precise moment he had mentally conceded it was to be Jacklin's Open.

Without ever hitting the fairway Trevino eventually found himself, four shots played, in the rough behind the green and still 40 ft from the flag.

Jacklin, who had played this long par five perfectly, had a chip and a putt for a birdie but his chip was a woefully weak effort, a good 20 ft short.

Trevino, still mentally beaten, took no time at all. A quick look at the half-buried ball, a nonchalant, almost casual swing and up and out it popped to roll and roll across the green and straight into the cup for an unbelievable par five.

For the fourth time Trevino had holed from off the green yet, all was not lost. Jacko still had two putts for the five that would have kept them level. Instead, he went for the birdie, charged his first putt four feet past the hole then missed the return for three putts and a shattering six.

Trevino, of course, went on to clinch the title on the final hole, pipping Jacklin by one shot for the round and two for the championship. In the space of 20 minutes certain triumph for Jacklin had turned to heartbreaking disaster and became, in my view, at least, the tragic turning point in Jacklin's brilliant, but all-too-short playing career.

The Second Coming of Jacko saw him once again in the front line, 20 years after receiving Henry Cotton's Rookie of the Year award. He was headlines again, captaining the Europe Ryder Cup team against America in Florida. His counterpart – that most respected of all adversaries, Jack Nicklaus.

To say the Europeans gave Nicklaus a fright would be the understatement of all time. For a while it looked as though Nicklaus, the mighty "Golden Bear", was to become the first American captain to lose a series on home soil. On the last day, with ten of the 12 singles matches completed, the teams were locked 13-13.

Canizares, at one stage three up against that redoubtable fighter, Lanny Wadkins, was still one up standing on the final tee. Bernard Gallacher, battling as always, was one down to the brilliant Tom Watson standing on the 17th. Bernie lost that hole to go down two and one to the man generally acknowledged to be, in 1983, if not the best in the world, not very far from it.

Wadkins, as he has on so many occasions, produced the killer stroke just when it was needed – a 70 yard pitch to within 15 inches of the final hole for a winning birdie and the vital half that gave the Americans their one point victory, $14\frac{1}{2}$-$13\frac{1}{2}$, with the very last shot of the series.

That was a marvellous beginning to The Second Coming and one which Jacklin himself rates as a remarkable triumph. Surely, more would follow. It did – at The Belfry.

Jacklin refuses to take credit for that triumph claiming all the kudos belongs to the players. "They did the job," he says, "and if anyone wants to give me any credit, O.K. But I am not deluding myself . . . the players won the Ryder Cup. Not me."

That is a generous, but over-modest, reaction. Jacklin's contribution was enormous and was frankly recognised by Peter Jacobsen, a million dollar winner on the US tour and a member of the beaten American team.

Said Peter, the man who rugby-tackled the streaker on the 18th green at the 1985 Open (and will probably be remembered more for that than for his creditable 11th place finish): "Tony was great, a true gentleman, understanding and encouraging. He was always on the course urging his team on. Europe should keep him as captain for the next 30 years – or give him to us!"

To that tribute I can add Jacklin was simply superb. He began by handsomely winning the psychological battle with Trevino when, at the flag-raising ceremony, he introduced his team . . . "Severiano Ballesteros, the greatest golfer in the world . . . Sandy Lyle . . . The Open champion . . . Bernhard Langer . . . US Masters champion . . ."

Jacklin introduces Ballesteros – "the greatest golfer in the world"

The pride shone through as Jacko reminded the visitors that Europe had all the aces in their pack. The message got through and the Americans slumped lower and lower in their seats.

Jacko, having built a closely-knit community at their Belfry quarters, made a point of conducting man-to-man chats with his players. One told him that he was feeling a bit down because he felt the newspapers were always having a go at him, giving him a hard time.

Jacko listened then quietly suggested the player didn't know what a hard time was. "I had it for years", Jacko told him. "If I didn't shoot below par every round, or win every tournament, I was labelled a failure."

Jacklin went on to tell how a newspaperman whom he had always regarded as a friend ended a review of his recent book – *Tony Jacklin, The First Forty Years* (MacDonald Queen Anne Press, £9.95) – with the words, following his fall from the top flight as a player, "What a wasted talent."

Pointing to his lower abdomen, Jacklin told the player: "Those words got me right here. But do you know what? Twenty-four hours after that article appeared the same newspaperman was on the telephone to me asking a favour. What did I do? I did the favour."

I know that tale to be true because I was the newspaperman.

On the course Jacklin follows every turn of fate

21

Jacko's final advice to the player . . . "Get your head down and prove them all wrong."

His immense contribution to that marvellous victory stemmed from his own personality and the respect that was automatic from a group of golfers who were willing to listen to a man who had trodden paths of glory few of them could hope to emulate. To those who had . . . Ballesteros, Langer and Lyle . . . the respect was even greater for here was one of golf's greatest performers showing every minute of the day and night that he cared and cared deeply, for their well-being and for their success. And to such an extent that he called on every caddy before the start of the final day singles to tell them: "You have got a big part to play. Keep telling your man how good he is. Talk positively. Keep him up."

In that respect Jacklin found close on 25,000 allies a day in those charged-up galleries. Their enthusiasm and their ear-shattering support left no doubts that, on this occasion certainly, European golfers were the best in the world.

Next chapter in The Second Coming of Tony Jacklin should be written in 1987 from the aptly named Muirfield, the course Jack Nicklaus built in America.

Good sense is possibly urging Jacko to quit while he is ahead. The competitor in him will be niggling: "Wouldn't it be something to captain the first winning European team on American soil."

Jacko would never be so presumptious as to ask for that chance. Golf would never be able to forgive itself if it didn't offer it to him. That would be the perfect finale.

2 History of the Ryder Cup

by Ron Wills

In 1926, Britain was gripped by the National Strike, and in June that year only a handful of people had the time or the inclination to take much notice of an unofficial, knock-about golf match at Wentworth.

The fact that Britain's professionals beat their American counterparts in a two day match by 13½ points to 1½ was reported fully in the Top People's newspaper, *The Times*, but created little or no impact elsewhere. It was an era when golf was considered the preserve of the wealthy and privileged.

But, thanks to two men – Samuel Ryder and the American golfing legend Walter Hagen – that match, that victory spawned one of the sport's most cherished traditions – the Ryder Cup.

Hagen had won the 1922 Open championship at Sandwich, and repeated his success at Hoylake in 1924. Those triumphs inspired and launched an annual invasion of American golfers. If Hagen had won it, it must be worth winning was their thinking, and suddenly every U.S. golfer was hungry to have his name engraved on golf's oldest Open trophy.

It was an invasion that forced the Open Championship's organisers, the Royal and Ancient, to re-think their policy. By 1926, there were so many entries, the R & A introduced qualifying rounds to be played before the Open Championship to decide which players should play in the event.

There were no exemptions in those days, and America's invading golfers were alloted Sunningdale as the venue for their qualifying competition. It meant of course the Americans had to make their trans-Atlantic trek earlier than normal, and with time to spare they agreed to form a team to play Britain's top professionals at nearby Wentworth.

Among the crowd who watched the match was Ryder, the son of a market gardener, who had set up his own business in St. Albans selling penny packets of seeds. It was a business that earned a fortune for Ryder, who was such a golfing enthusiast he employed Abe Mitchell, one of Britain's top players, as his own personal coach. Mitchell beat the reigning U.S. Open champion Jim Barnes eight and seven in the singles, and then partnered George Duncan in the foursomes to beat Hagen and Barnes nine and eight.

Ryder was so impressed, he put up the now famous, solid golf trophy for regular competition between the two nations ... and the Ryder Cup was born.

Sam Ryder presents his 1929 trophy to winning Great Britain Captain
George Duncan

The first official match was organised for June 1927, in Worcester, Massachusets, but if the cost of the trophy was, by present days standards, inexpensive – around £250 – the price of sending Britain's eight man team to the U.S.A. was not. Around £3,000 was needed, and to get it the magazine *Golf Illustrated* launched a public appeal. Ryder himself donated £100. The R & A sent £50. The Stock Exchange golfing society weighed in with £200. And for reasons best known to themselves, one London company donated the princely sum of 6s7d – that's about 33p in today's decimal currency.

The Editor of *Golf Illustrated*, George Philpot, wrote at the time: "I want the appeal to be successful because it will give British professionals a chance to avenge the defeats which have been adminstered by American Professionals while visiting our shores in search of Open Championship honours.

"I know that, given a fair chance, our fellows can and will bring back the Cup from America. But they must have a fair chance, which means that adequate money must be found to finance the trip. Can the money be found? The answer rests with the British golfing public." The answer was "Yes". By early April the fund had reached £2,178-13-1d – nobody knows where the odd penny came from – and the match was "on".

The British team, captained by Ted Ray, who had won the 1920 U.S. Open, sailed from Southampton on board the liner Aquitania with high hopes of repeating their Wentworth triumph. They came home from Worcester, home town of world middleweight champion Marvin Hagler, having received a hammering.

The Americans won by 9½ points to 2½, with George Duncan scoring Britain's only singles victory. Hagen got his revenge, too. He beat the 1923 Open champion Arthur Havers two and one.

In spite of that defeat, Havers has fond memories of the match, and his clash with Hagen. Havers once told me: "The whole thing about going to America was a culture shock for most of us. When we got to New York, the entire team and the officials were whisked through without bothering about customs and immigration formalities.

"There was a fleet of limousines waiting for us at the dockside. And, with police outriders flanking us with their sirens on full blast, we sped through New York. Traffic was halted to let us through – it was a whole new world for us. Everywhere we went, we were overwhelmed by the hospitality and kindness of the Americans. Suddenly, we were in a world of luxury and plenty – so different from home. It was something we had never expected. Even the club houses were luxurious with deep pile carpets, not like the often run down and shabby club houses at home which is all most of us really knew".

Hagen may have beaten him two and one, but Havers recalls "There was never more than a hole in it either way until we got to the 17th – and then I was beaten by a stymie". Unlike today, players in 1927 were not able to mark their balls on the green. If an opponent's ball was between a player and the hole, he either had to play over it or around it.

Added Havers: "I tried to putt my ball around Hagen's, but it hit it instead and shot off at an angle, six or seven feet away from the hole. I missed that putt and when Hagen holed his, he went two up – and that was the match. But I'll never forget playing with him. He was a larger than life man – a character, a real personality. A great showman.

"And I'll never forget the famous phrase he coined – 'You're only here for a short time. Don't worry, don't hurry – and don't forget to stop and smell the roses on the way.'."

It was Hagen who also once said: "I don't want to be a millionaire – I just want to live like one". He did, too. He also dabbled in the stock market, and was almost ruined in the 1929 Wall Street crash.

But he always bounced back, and was such a force in American golf he captained every U.S. team in the Ryder Cup matches prior to World War II, and played in all but one of them.

Havers, however, did get his revenge for that defeat in the inaugural match. In 1931, in Ohio, Havers partnered George Duncan in the foursomes and they scored a massive 10 and nine victory against Hagen and Denny Shute.

That, however, is jumping ahead. Philpot, the *Golf Illustrated* editor, managed the British team in that opening match in 1927, and his comments later were to become the British lament throughout Ryder Cup matches right up until the modern era.

Said Philpot: "We were outputted. They (the Americans) didn't beat us off the tee, or in the long iron shots, but they were rather better than us in the shots from 80 yards and under, and definitely superior when it came to holing out with the putter."

In May 1929 – five months before the Wall Street crash – Hagen's Heroes defended the trophy at Moortown (Leeds) – and failed.

Hagen won his foursomes match, but was hammered 10 and eight by George Duncan in the singles ... the first and last time he ever lost a Ryder Cup singles match.

Britain's victory was aided by a fresh-faced young professional of 22 who beat Al Watrous four and three in the singles. His

The great Walter Hagen receives the 1937 Ryder Cup on behalf of the U.S.A.

name? The legendary Henry Cotton who went on to win the Open championship three times.

Cotton, who now lives at Penina, Portugal, where he designed what is arguably the finest golf course on the Algarve, once told me: "Golf is really a selfish game most of the time.

"Professionals play it for money and do everything they can to beat their fellow professionals every time they step on to the first tee.

"But there's something about the Ryder Cup that brings out the team spirit in golfers. Maybe it's the prospect of beating the Americans, who for so long have been the kings of golf.

"Maybe it's a throw back to their schooldays when team sports, and not individual sports, were the most important aspect of games. I don't know. But I do know that golfers who normally want only to beat their rivals become, that week, the best of pals."

A perfect example of that occurred when the 1985 team was finalised. About three weeks before the match, non-playing skipper Tony Jacklin told Ian Woosnam he would be partnering Paul Way in the foursomes and/or fourball matches.

Way had won his place in the European team with early season displays, including winning the PGA Championship in a play-off against Sandy Lyle. But in the weeks leading up to the Ryder Cup, his performances had slumped, and he had missed the half-way qualifying cut in six of the seven tournaments in which he played.

Under normal circumstances, that would have been his problem – and his alone. But Woosnam said: "As soon as Tony told me, I went out with Paul in an effort to sort out his game. If he was going to be my partner in the Ryder Cup I was willing to do anything I could to help sort out his problems".

But that, once again, is jumping way ahead. Back in 1931, Britain, once more the proud holders of the Ryder Cup, travelled to Columbus, Ohio, to defend the title – and yet again came home empty handed.

The Americans won nine-three. In 1933, J.H. Taylor was appointed non-playing captain of the British team to face the U.S.A. at Southport, and he promptly demanded his team should be at a peak of fitness. To achieve it, he hired a physical training instructor who put the British team through a rigorous training routine – which included a run along the beach at Southport every morning at 6.30.

It worked – but only just. A crowd of 15,000, a record at the time, watched the final day's singles, though some of them were not too sure about what they were watching. Among the crowd was the Prince of Wales, (later Edward VIII) who was a golfing enthusiast, and it's suspected some of the crowd were there to see him rather than the action.

The British team was without Cotton, who had won the first of his three Open titles in 1934, because he had taken a job at the Waterloo club in Belgium. Under the rules at that time he was not eligible to be selected because he wasn't attached to a club in the United Kingdom.

Even without him, Britain won the first day foursomes by $2\frac{1}{2}$ points to $1\frac{1}{2}$, but the Americans hit back the following day, winning four of the eight singles, and victories by Abe Mitchell, Percy Alliss and Arthur Havers earned three points for Britain.

That meant the two sides were dead level, with five and a half points each, and even if some of the spectators didn't realise it at the time, it meant the match's outcome was all down to the final singles in what was arguably one of the most exciting finishes in Ryder Cup history.

The two men involved were Britain's Syd Easterbrook and Denny Shute, and to add to the tension they were all-square after

35 holes. Nerves and pressure were obviously a key factor, and neither could handle it – both put their drives into bunkers, and both took three shots to reach the green. It was Eastbrook's turn to putt first, and it was Eastbrook who conquered the pressure best.

He left his approach putt stone dead for a five, but Shute three-putted from closer range – and Britain had won again, by six and a half points to five and a half.

It also meant Britain and America were level in the series two-two – both nations having won twice on home ground. That, however, was the end of the level-pegging situation.

In 1935, the British team which included the three Whitcombe brothers – Charles, Reg and Ernest – went to New Jersey and lost nine-three. It was to be another 22 years before the Americans had the Ryder Cup wrenched from their grasp.

The Americans returned to Britain in 1937, and at Southport in June scored the first victory on foreign soil in the history of the Ryder Cup, winning eight-four and so began the long series of American triumphs on both sides of the Atlantic.

The Americans selected a team for the 1939 match, but by the time it was scheduled to be played, Britain had other battles on its mind, and the trophy donated by seed merchant Ryder, who had died in 1936, stood proudly locked away in the headquarters of the U.S. PGA.

The series was renewed in 1947, but after six years of war and still in the midst of austerity and food rationing, Britain's golfers were in no shape to offer more than a token resistance. In Portland, Oregon, in November of that year they were on the painful end of crushing 11-one defeat – Sam King's four and three singles victory earned the solitary point – against an American side which included golfing legends such as Sam Snead and Byron Nelson.

It was the start of a long, depressing series as far as British golf was concerned. The Americans steamrollered their way through the opposition to record victory after victory. They won seven-five at Ganton in 1949, and by a massive nine and a half points to two and a half in North Carolina two years later.

The 1949 match did produce one of the first rows in the series when the U.S.A.'s captain Ben Hogan – still suffering from the affects of his car crash – complained about the groovings on the clubs of some of the British players.

The problem was solved with what was described at the time as "a little filing", but an incensed British team promptly went out and established an opening day lead of three-one in the foursomes. It was the perfect launching pad for a victory, but the

Americans hit back in the singles, winning six of the eight matches – Dai Rees and Jimmy Adams were Britain's only two players to succeed.

Henry Cotton captained the British team for the only time in 1953 when the match was staged at Wentworth, and he, too, was involved in controversy.

The U.S.A. won the foursomes three-one, and an angry Cotton made the mistake of voicing his frustration when he said of his team: "I could kick them". The comment was a sub-editor's delight, and immediately became a sporting page headline and the subject of newspaper placards.

They were liberally distributed around Wentworth the following day, and Cotton's late wife, the volatile Toots, went around the club-house area ripping up the placards in front of puzzled newspaper sellers.

In spite of that start, the British team fought back bravely in the singles – none more than Harry Weetman who beat Snead at the 36th hole after being four down with six holes to play.

In the end, the match result rested on the young shoulders of 22-year-old Peter Alliss, who had followed his father's footsteps into the Ryder Cup team and was playing in his first match. He needed to halve his match with Jim Turnsea to earn a tie.

One down with one to play he missed the green with his approach, and then fluffed the chip to give Turnsea a one hole victory. It was a short game problem that was to trouble Allis for the rest of his life. He once told me: "I feel I've had to live my whole life with the guilt of messing up that chip".

An eight-four victory for the Americans followed in California in 1955, and yet another defeat looked on the cards when the Americans took a three-one lead in foursomes at Lindrick in October 1957.

Instead, Britain's team produced a devastating display of golf and an epic turnaround to pull off what was the most astonishing victory in Ryder Cup history.

Eric Brown, the gritty Scot who was never beaten in a Ryder Cup singles match, gave the team a magnificent start with a four and three success against Tommy Bolt. The British victory charge was on, though nobody dared believe it to begin with. Slowly, it dawned on the crowd that, for once, another American victory was not inevitable.

One by one, the British victories were totted up. Peter Mills now a reinstated amateur living in Jersey, beat Jackie Burke five and three. Skipper Rees hammered Ed Furgol seven and six. Ireland's Christy O'Connor won by the same margin against Dow

Finsterwald, and Bernard Hunt was just behind them with a six and five victory over Doug Ford.

And, suddenly, it was all down to Ken Bousfield . . . and he obliged with a four and three win against Lionel Herbert.

Even in triumph, however, there was controversy. Team captain Rees dropped 1951 Open champion Max Faulkner and Harry Weetman, who had lost their foursomes match, from the singles. An angry and upset Weetman created his own headlines when he announced: "I'll never play in a team captained by Rees again."

By contrast, the gregarious Faulkner spent the second day of the match racing around the course, sometimes literally running, passing on news of other matches and generally boosting the morale of British players, telling them all individually that they could and would win their matches.

Weetman was later disciplined for his outburst, while Faulkner to this day is remembered for his inspiration.

Bousfield, who clinched victory, said: "Those were the days before scoreboards out on the course and walkie-talkies. All of us playing out there would have had no idea what was happening in the other matches if it wasn't for Max. He was marvellous. And he seemed to bring good news every time I saw him. He'd nip up to me between shots and say: 'Rees is winning.' . . . 'Brown's four up.' . . . 'We've got them on the run, Guvnor.' 'Go on! You can beat this boy'.

"Then he'd dash off and come back ten minutes later with more good news. We might have won without him, but he was magnificent that day – I'll never forget what he did."

The euphoria lasted for two years – and then it was back to the inevitable reality. In November 1959, the Americans got their revenge with an eight and a half to three and a half victory in California.

The Ryder Cup format was changed in 1961 when the match came to Royal Lytham. Matches were reduced from 36 holes to 18 holes, allowing for both a morning and an afternoon session and with more points at stake. It made no different to the outcome. The U.S.A. won that match 14½-9½, and they went on winning. By 23-9 in 1963 in Atlanta, when four ball matches were introduced for the first time, by 19½-12½ at Royal Birkdale in 1965, and by 23½-8½ at Houston in 1967.

There was a hiccup in America's victory march in 1969 though when a British team, no doubt boosted by Tony Jacklin's breakthrough Open Championship victory that year, snatched a draw in one of the series' most gripping climaxes.

The two teams were dead level with the two final singles still out on the course. In the first, the gutsy little Welshman Brian

In the audience of around seven million viewers – a TV record for golf – who tuned in to watch the dramatic and emotional final afternoon's play in the 1985 Ryder Cup, one man more than any other understood Sam Torrance's delight.

Ken Bousfield, the last player to have won the Ryder Cup for Britain.

Torrance's putt rolled back the years for 66-year-old Bousfield to that October afternoon at Lindrick in Yorkshire in 1957. Bousfield was a member of that triumphant team, and it was his putt for a four and three victory over the reigning U.S. PGA champion Lionel Herbert that sealed America's defeat.

He recalls: "The one big difference from Torrance's was that my match finished out in the country, on the 15th green. But it was the same sort of emotion. I can understand Sam crying. I didn't in 1957 – but I felt like it. I was cheered and applauded all the way as I walked back to the club house. I can still hear them now – it was a wonderful day in my life, one I'll never forget.

"We didn't have the sophisticated scoring systems they have today, and we didn't have the scoreboards out on the course. But the bush telegraph system was almost as effective. Our captain Dai Rees certainly knew what was going on. He joined me at the 15th hole and told me if I finished off Herbert we had won the match.

"It was a par four, and I rolled up my approach putt a bit short – about 18 inches away. I looked enquiringly at Herbert hoping I would get the nod, that he would concede. But he just looked at me and said: 'One more time, Kenny, one more time'. Thankfully it went in, and after that all I could remember was the cheers, the back slapping, the congratulations as I walked back to the club house."

Huggett was playing Billy Casper. Huggett needed to hold a four putt to halve his match, and was interrupted as he stood over the putt by a tremendous roar from the crowd surrounding the 17th green.

He immediately and understandably thought it signalled victory for Jacklin in his match against Jack Nicklaus. It wasn't – the cheer was for a Jacklin eagle that put him level with Nicklaus with one hole to play.

But Huggett, after holing the putt, thought it had given Britain a victory in the match and he burst into tears as he fell into the arms of non-playing captain Eric Brown. That was only the start of the drama. Jacklin and Nicklaus both reached the final

The 1957 victory was the first since 1933 when Britain's team was captained by the legendary J.H. Taylor at Southport and Ainsdale, but Bousfield recalls his squad weren't surprised at their victory.

"It might have come as a surprise to a lot of people, even people in golf," he said, "but the mood of the team was 'We can do it'. Even after we lost the foursomes three and one on the opening day we still felt confident as we talked about the match over dinner that evening.

"Remember we played only four foursomes matches and eight singles in those days, so we had a lot of ground to make up. We must have been a stubborn lot, maybe a bit arrogant, but whatever the reason the feeling was the match could still be won. Few people in golf were more arrogant than Eric Brown, and he gave us a great start by beating Tommy Bolt four and three in the opening match – just as Manuel Pinero gave Europe a great start by beating Lanny Wadkins this year.

"From then on we just rolled from one victory to another. Peter Mills beat Jackie Burke five and three, Dai Rees and Christy O'Connor both scored massive seven and six victories and Bernhard Hunt won six and five. Then came my moment – the moment I'll never forget."

Bousfield still plays three or four times a week, and still manages to shoot scores in the low 70's. "I suppose I play to a two or three handicap these days. I can still drive the ball just about as far as I did when I was a tournament golfer. But I can't will the putts in like I used to. The concentration goes very easily, so does the nerve.

"But I still love it. Golf keeps me alive – and I'm still looking for the secret of how to master the game. I don't suppose I'll ever find it now . . . but I'll always have the memory of that wonderful day."

green in two. Jacklin was the first to putt, and left his ball two feet short of the hole.

Then it was Nicklaus' turn, and his ball slid four feet past the hole. The tension was unbearable for the huge crowd. It was worse for the players. Nicklaus lined up his return putt and amid total silence holed it.

That left Jacklin with his two footer to halve the entire match, but we'll never know if he would have made it or not. Nicklaus, with a tremendous show of sportsmanship, bent down, picked up Jacklin's ball and conceded the putt.

Jacklin recalls the incident and says: "At first I could hardly believe what was happening. Then I said to Jack: 'I could have missed that'. His reply was typical of the man. He said: 'Maybe, but I doubt it. Anyway I wouldn't let you do that in front of all these people'.

"But that's Jack Nicklaus all over. He's a great man, a great golfer as his record proves, but most of all a great man. An example came a few minutes before he conceded that putt. As we walked from the 18th tee, both of us acutely aware of the position in the match, he called me over, put his arm around my shoulder and said: 'Are you nervous, Tony?'

"I told him I was shaking like a leaf. He smiled and said: 'Well, if it's any consolation. So am I'."

The match was tied 16-16, and the famous gold trophy was shared, with each country holding it for 12 months.

If nothing else, that tie proved that the gap between British and American golf was slowly, very slowly, beginning to close. Eric Brown again captained the 1971 team in St. Louis and although they lost the five point margin it was the best display by a British team on American soil up to that point in the Ryder Cup.

The gap was six points when the Americans won at Muirfield in 1973, a year when Scotland's Bernard Gallacher was struck down with food poisoning after partnering Brian Barnes to victory in the foursomes against Lee Trevino and Billy Casper, a victory that helped give Britain a five and a half to two and a half lead.

The Americans won the 1975 at Laurel Valley, Pennsylvania, comfortably, by 21 points to 11, a defeat that softened on the final day when Brian Barnes beat Nicklaus twice in singles matches, by four and two in the morning and two and one in the afternoon.

The gap wasn't closing fast enough, though, for the Americans and when they won yet again at Royal Lytham in 1977 the rumblings of discontent grew louder – and were voiced by Nicklaus.

In 1975, the U.S. PGA had persuaded a reluctant American TV network to screen the match live, but the TV top brass were furious when the outcome of the match was decided before they went on the air to show the final afternoon's session of singles.

Two years later, after the American victory at Lytham, Nicklaus said: "The American golfers are quite happy to treat this match as a goodwill gesture, a get together, a bit of fun. But here in Britain it's treated differently. The people here seem to want a serious, knock-em-down match. If that's what's wanted, there has to be stronger opposition. Something has to be done to make it more of a match for the Americans."

Nicklaus, because of his standing in the game, wasn't without clout, and he passed on his views to the U.S. PGA when the team returned home. The U.S. PGA took the point, and still smarting from their humiliation with American TV in 1975, began delicate negotiations to improve the standard of opposition.

European golf had grown rapidly in the early 1970's, and it was finally agreed the team should represent the European circuit, which would allow players other than British to play in the team.

In 1979, Europe's 12 man squad included ten British golfers and two Spaniards – Severiano Ballesteros, who had won his first Open title earlier that year, and Antonio Garrido.

The inclusion of Europeans made little difference to begin with. America won that 1979 match in West Virginia 17-11, and Ballesteros, in spite of being the reigning Open champion, was beaten an astonishing four times in five outings – and all the American victories involved Larry Nelson who took his own personal Ryder Cup record to: "Played nine, won nine."

Ballesteros and Garrido partnered each other in two sessions of foursomes and two sessions of fourballs, and won only once – beating Fuzzy Zoeller and Hubert Green three and two. In the singles, the draw put Ballesteros and Nelson together yet again, and the Spaniard lost yet again, by three and two.

Ballesteros didn't play in the 1981 match. A squabble over appearance money meant he didn't compete in sufficient tournaments to play his way into the team, and the selectors declined to include him among the three selected players.

The West German Bernhard Langer joined two other Spaniards, Jose-Maria Canizares and Manuel Pinero in the 1981 line-up, but even the presence of Ballesteros, by then recognised as one of the world's outstanding golfing talents, is unlikely to have altered the result.

The U.S. team, which won 18½-9½ at Walton Heath, was unquestionably the most awesome and talented squad of golfers ever assembled. The line-up read like a golfing Debrett of the time.

It included three of the four major championship winners that year – Tom Watson (U.S. Masters), the golfer with the Indian sign on Ballesteros, Larry Nelson (U.S. PGA), and Open champion Bill Rogers.

As if that wasn't enough, there was also multiple major championship winners Lee Trevino, Ray Floyd, Jack Nicklaus and Johnny Miller. It looked an unbeatable squad – and it was. The American team was on song, too, as Tom Kite proved when he played Sandy Lyle in the singles. Lyle had eight birdies in his round – by anyone's standards quality golf. But it wasn't enough. Kite had ten, and romped to a three and two victory.

That peak, however, also marked the end of America's dominance. Tony Jacklin was non-playing captain of the 1983 European side that went to Florida . . . a side that gave the Americans the fright of their lives.

The U.S.A.'s non-playing captain was Jack Nicklaus who seemed to sense the Ryder Cup balance of power was swinging towards Europe when he said before the match: "If the Europeans are going to win here in America they'll never have a better chance than they have this year."

He was nearly right. Europe led by a point after the opening day, and trailed by a point after day two. That meant it was all down to the final day's 12 singles matches.

Ballesteros got a half against Zoeller in the opening singles, and then the match swung to Europe thanks to victories by Nick Faldo, who beat Jay Haas two and one, and Langer who triumphed by two holes against Gil Morgan.

At one point on that hot, steamy afternoon Europe led in all the remaining matches. But with ten of the singles settled, Europe and the U.S.A. were locked in a tie – 13-13. The outcome depended on Canizares who, after being three up at one stage, was one up on the 18th tee against Lanny Wadkins, and Gallacher one down to Watson on the 17th tee.

But victory was cruelly snatched from Europe's grasp. Gallacher missed a six foot putt at the 17th to give Watson a two and one win, and Wadkins conjured up a miracle wedge shot from 70 yards to within 15 inches of the hole for a birdie to halve with Canizares.

The final result, a $14\frac{1}{2}$-$13\frac{1}{2}$ victory for the Americans. But they knew how close they had been to losing for the first time on their own soil.

A very relieved Nicklaus led the American players out on to the course to embrace Wadkins after his winning shot at the final hole – and Nicklaus even knelt down to kiss the turf from the point Wadkins had played the shot.

Nicklaus had got what he wanted – a real match. The Europeans were, naturally, disappointed, but they were no longer over-awed by the Americans, no longer accepted that an American victory was ordained.

They had lost, but the scent of victory was in their nostrils. It was a scent that turned to the sweet smell of success on that glorious September day at The Belfry in 1985.

3   *European Team: Who's Who*

by Mitchell Platts

SEVERIANO BALLESTEROS
Born: April 9, 1957, Pedrena, Spain.
Lives: Pedrena, Spain.
Height: 6-0. Weight: 177.
Turned Pro: 1974.

Career Highlights
Ryder Cup: 1979, 1983.
British Open: 1979, 1984.
U.S. Masters: 1980, 1983.
Dutch Open: 1976, 1980.
Lancome Trophy: 1976, 1983.
French Open: 1977, 1982, 1985.
Uniroyal International: 1977.
Japanese Open: 1977, 1978.
Dunlop Phoenix (Japan): 1977, 1981.
Otago Classic (New Zealand): 1977.
Swiss Open: 1977, 1978.
Martini International: 1978, 1980.
German Open: 1978.
Scandinavian Open: 1978, 1981.
Kenya Open: 1978.

Greater Greensboro Open (U.S.): 1978.
English Golf Classic: 1979.
Madrid Open: 1980, 1982.
Spanish Open: 1981.
Suntory World Match Play Championship: 1981, 1982, 1984, 1985.
Australian PGA Championship: 1981.
Westchester Classic (U.S.): 1983.
Sun City Challenge (S.A.): 1983, 1984.
PGA Championship: 1983.
Carrolls Irish Open: 1983, 1985.
USF & G Classic (U.S.): 1985.
Sanyo Open: 1985.

Severiano Ballesteros made an inauspicious start to his Ryder Cup career. When the door was opened to the continentals – in 1979 – he joined Spanish compatriot Antonio Garrido in the team. The pair managed only one point from four games then Ballesteros lost three and two to Larry Nelson in the singles. Then, two years later, Ballesteros, following an altercation with the tour, was not selected. He came back, however, in 1983 and there is no doubt that he brought to the "dressing room" inspired confidence simply by having proved that the Americans could be beaten in their own backyard.

Ballesteros had won the U.S. Masters in 1980 and 1983 and he was by now the world's number one golfer. The rest of the team drew confidence from the Spaniard's achievements and with Tony Jacklin's inspiration the Europeans came within a whisker of success in Florida. The coincidence is that Ballesteros has turbocharged the European scene since Jacklin's demise as a player and together the pair have such infectious belief in themselves that they were able to galvanise every team member at The Belfry.

Ballesteros initially forged his links with the game, like so many Spaniards, by caddying . . . although he was fortunate in that the family's 19th century farmhouse home overlooked the Real Club de Golf de Pedrena on Spain's northern coast. There Ballesteros struck his first shots, aged seven, with a club fashioned from a rusting three iron head, hand-fitted into a stick acting as a shaft. And he used stones, collected from the beach, as balls.

His progress was swift. He played nine holes in 51 shots at the age of ten then two years later he posted a 79 to win the caddie championship. He became, at the age of 16 years and eight months, the youngest accredited professional in Spanish golf history since when his astonishing achievements have been well documented.

KEN BROWN
Born: January 9th, 1957, Harpenden, Herts, England.
Lives: Harpenden, Herts, England.
Height: 6-2. Weight: 151.
Turned Pro: 1974.

Career Highlights
Ryder Cup: 1977, 1979, 1983, 1985.
Carrolls Irish Open: 1978.
KLM Dutch Open: 1983.
Kenya Open: 1983.
Glasgow Open: 1984.
Four Stars National
    Pro-Celebrity: 1985.

38

Ken Brown's determination to reach the top of his profession can be gauged by the amount of time he has spent these past two years in the United States. It has not been easy for Brown, constantly flying back and forth across the Atlantic, and it has most certainly been a costly mission. Not only have his expenses been high but he has also missed out on bigger profits in Europe where he might have been winning more and earning places in such events as the Dunhill Cup.

Even so, Brown is satisfied because he is convinced that his golf game has improved through regular competition against the likes of Curtis Strange, Lanny Wadkins and Tom Watson. Moreover he prefers the courses in America and the superb practice facilities.

Brown also showed his resilience in 1984. He had gained his players' card, for the U.S. circuit, by qualifying through the school but he was in danger of losing it after only one season. To survive he had to finish third or better in the last event, the Pensacola Open, and to his credit Brown led after three rounds and finished joint second.

In common with his colleagues Brown has the conventional ambition of wanting to win the Open Championship. He believes that playing in America has improved his prospects. And he is convinced that, unlike at Muirfield in 1980 when he lost an outside chance after moving into second place at the 54-hole stage, if he gets in that position again he will be able to cope with the pressure.

He has certainly risen to the occasion in past Ryder Cups with singles wins over Fuzzy Zoeller and Ray Floyd.

JOSE-MARIA CANIZARES
Born: February 18th, 1947, Madrid, Spain.
Lives: Madrid, Spain.
Height: 5-10. Weight: 158.
Turned Pro: 1967.

Career Highlights
Ryder Cup: 1981, 1983, 1985.
World Cup: 1974, 1980, 1982 (winner with Manuel Pinero), 1983, 1984 (winner with Jose Rivero).

World Cup Individual Winner: 1984.
Jersey Open: 1980.
Bob Hope British Classic: 1980, 1983.
Italian Open: 1981.
Kenya Open: 1984.

Jose-Maria Canizares earned more than £125,000 in official golf winnings in 1984 . . . but he never won a tournament in Europe. The staggering sum, boosted by six top ten finishes on the European tour, came about with the help of a victory in the Kenya Open then a truly superb win in the World Cup. Canizares and Jose Rivero teamed up to give Spain victory in Rome – earning them £24,000 each – and Canizares walked off with the individual winner's first prize of £20,000 as well.

The surprising fact is that Canizares does not win more often. Not only is he one of the most consistent golfers on the tour but he is also capable of producing the kind of marvellous scoring streaks which usually launch players to victories. In the 1978 Swiss Open, on the switchback Crans-sur-Seine course, he ended his second round with five consecutive birdies then followed the next day with six straight birdies and an eagle. That equalled a world record and he set a European record with an outward nine hole score of 27 in that third round.

Even so he must be more than satisfied. Canizares was compelled to leave school at the age of ten to become a caddie because of the family's need for money. His father was a bricklayer and Jose-Maria was one of seven children – four boys and three daughters. It was an austere childhood that has enabled him to keep his feet firmly on the ground. The slim, elegant Spaniard has certainly done just that.

HOWARD CLARK
Born: August 26, 1954, Leeds, Yorkshire, England.
Lives: Leeds.
Height: 6-1. Weight 182.
Turned Pro: 1973.

Career Highlights
Ryder Cup: 1977, 1981, 1985.
Walker Cup: 1973.
World Cup: 1984.
Portuguese Open: 1978.
Madrid Open: 1978, 1984.
Whyte and Mackay PGA
  Championship: 1984.
Jersey Open: 1985.

Howard Clark has come a long way since his formative years when he lived with his mother, grandmother and uncle in a back-to-back house not far from the jail in Armley, Leeds. But his progress as a professional was blunted for a time as he was often imprisoned by his own lack of resilience when fortune swung against him.

What transformed Clark from journeyman to winner in 1978 – he captured the Portuguese and Madrid Opens in a three week spell – was some wise counselling from the experienced Peter Alliss who pointed out to Clark the need for him to control his temperament.

There was no doubt about Clark's potential. He had won the British Boys', moved onto the youth internationals then graduated to the Walker Cup. His double success in the summer of 1978, in his fifth year of playing for pay, made him an overnight star. He climbed to fifth in the Order of Merit – although he failed to win in the next five seasons.

Clark's comeback in 1984, when he was a double winner again, can be traced to his marriage to Beverley the previous November and to his own ability to restrain himself in troubled moments and accept that in golf there are many frustrating times when things do not go according to plan.

Victory in the Ryder Cup was especially nice for Howard since eight years earlier the match had led to one of his biggest disappointments. He could never understand why the public knew before him that he had not been selected for the fourballs, after missing the foursomes, and he was thrown in at number one in the singles against the aggressive Lanny Wadkins. Clark, however, demonstrated his fighting qualities in the 1981 match when he overcame Tom Watson in the singles – and he certainly contributed much to Europe's win in 1985.

NICK FALDO

Born: July 18, 1957, Welwyn Garden City, Hertfordshire, England.
Lives: Windlesham, Surrey, England.
Height: 6-3. Weight: 189.
Turned Pro: 1976.

Career Highlights
Ryder Cup: 1977, 1979, 1981, 1983, 1985.
Skol Lager: 1977.
PGA Championship: 1978, 1980, 1981.
ICL Tournament (S.A.): 1979.
Tournament Players Championship: 1982.
French Open: 1983.
Martini International: 1983.
Car Care Plan International: 1983, 1984.
Lawrence Batley International: 1983.
European Masters: 1983.
Sea Pines Heritage Classic (U.S.A.): 1984.

Nick Faldo's fifth successive appearance in the Ryder Cup was undoubtedly the most pleasurable at the end of the day, as he

41

joined the excited celebrations afterwards in the swimming pool, but the match unfolded as he was still seeking to complete a radical swing change designed to improve his striking.

So Faldo was unable to improve his Ryder Cup record – although it is a record which deserves close scrutiny for it accurately mirrors his enormous capabilities.

What Faldo achieved on his Ryder Cub debut at Royal Lytham and St. Annes in 1977 was nothing less than remarkable. He teamed up with Peter Oosterhuis to win his foursomes then the next day the same partnership brushed aside Jack Nicklaus and Ray Floyd three and one in the fourballs. Faldo, then only 20 years old, went out on day three to complete a hat-trick with a last green win against Tom Watson.

Faldo and Oosterhuis linked to win two out of three at The Greenbrier in 1979 – Faldo also won his singles – and Faldo made it three singles wins in a row when he overcame Johnny Miller in the 1981 match at Walton Heath. In 1983, at the PGA National Golf Club in Florida, Faldo joined forces with Bernhard Langer and they won three of their four matches. Then Faldo overcame Jay Haas in the singles.

Faldo enjoyed a superb amateur career, winning virtually everything in which he played in 1975, before he joined the professional ranks. He was in the Ryder Cup team before he made his big breakthrough on the European circuit – that came in 1978 when he powered his way to victory in the PGA Championship at Royal Birkdale. He was to capture that prestigious title twice more in the next three years – once at Royal St. George's – and his form on links courses suggests that, like Sandy Lyle, he will become an Open Championship winner.

Faldo enjoyed his best year in 1983 when he won five titles on the European tour. Since then he has campaigned for longer spells in the United States, where he won the Sea Pines Heritage Classic in 1984, and he has set his sights on becoming a regular winner across the Atlantic.

TONY JACKLIN (Non-Playing Captain)
Born: July 7, 1944, Scunthorpe, Lincolnshire, England.
Lives: Sotogrande, Spain.
Height: 5-9½. Weight: 168.
Turned Pro: 1962.

Career Highlights	1975, 1977, 1979,
Ryder Cup: 1967, 1969, 1971, 1973,	(non-playing captain) 1983, 1985.

British Open: 1969.
U.S. Open: 1970.
Pringle Tournament: 1967.
Dunlop Masters: 1967, 1973.
Forest Products (N.Z.): 1967.
New Zealand PGA Championship:
   1967.
Jacksonville Open (U.S.): 1968,
   1972.
WD & HO Wills Open: 1970.
Lancome Trophy: 1970.

Benson and Hedges Festival: 1971.
PGA Championship: 1972, 1982.
Dunlop International (Australia):
   1972.
Bogota Open: 1973.
Italian Open: 1973.
Los Lagartos Open: 1974.
Scandinavian Open: 1974.
Kerrygold International: 1976.
German Open: 1979.
Venezuelan Open: 1979.

A new chapter in Tony Jacklin's career began when he was invited to be Ryder Cup captain. The earlier chapters tell an extraordinary story . . . of the lorry driver's son from Scunthorpe whose own brilliance lit the touch fuse on a golfing explosion in Britain. Jacklin's victory in the British Open at Royal Lytham and St Annes in 1969 encouraged thousands upon thousands to take-up golf and subsequently led to a sponsorship boost which took the European circuit galloping to today's £5 million prize fund. (*See also* John Morgan's profile, page 13.)

BERNHARD LANGER
Born: August 27, 1957, Anhausen, West Germany.
Lives: Anhausen and Florida, U.S.A.
Height: 5-9. Weight: 156.
Turned Pro: 1972.

Career Highlights
Ryder Cup: 1981, 1983, 1985.
U.S. Masters: 1985.
World Cup: 1976, 1977, 1978, 1979,
   1980.
Cacharel Under 25's
   Championship: 1979.
Dunlop Masters: 1980.
Colombian Open: 1980.
German Open: 1981, 1982, 1985.
Bob Hope British Classic: 1981.
Italian Open: 1983.
Glasgow Classic: 1983.

Tournament Players
   Championship: 1983.
Johnnie Walker Trophy (Spain):
   1983.
Casio World Open (Japan): 1983.
French Open: 1984.
Dutch Open: 1984.
Carrolls Irish Open: 1984.
Spanish Open: 1984.
Australian Masters: 1985.
Sea Pines Heritage Classic
   (U.S.A.): 1985.
European Open: 1985.

Victory in the U.S. Masters was followed, one week later, by success in the Sea Pines Heritage Classic. Two victories in eight days on the American circuit – including one of the most coveted prizes in the game. For Bernhard Langer there must have been a moment at Augusta in April when his mind returned to a day at the Augsberg Golf Club, near where he grew up, when he boldly announced that he wanted to be a professional golfer. It was 1972, Langer knew little of such golfing heroes as Jack Nicklaus and Arnold Palmer, and, he confesses now, "My friends thought I was quite mad."

Langer, however, is a fighter. He has been from the start of his life. And he has pushed down one obstacle after another to rival Sevvy Ballesteros as the world's number one golfer. Bernhard's father, Erwin, a refugee from Sudetenland, a slice of Czechoslovakia, was caught by the Russians and put on a train which, presumably, was heading for Siberia. Langer says: "My father jumped the train. He was shot at – but he escaped."

Erwin eventually arrived in Anhausen, a hamlet in Bavaria, and he married. He earned his living as a bricklayer and there were three children – Bernhard being the youngest. Bernhard became mesmerised with golf from the moment he walked, as a nine-year-old, the five miles to the Augsburg club in the village of Burgwalden. There Bernhard caddied for the club champion. His ambition to be a professional became stronger and he obtained a position as assistant at the Munich Golf Club.

He served a three year apprenticeship before joining the European tour in 1976 – missing his first two halfway cuts then finishing joint fifth in the Madrid Open. But his career was immediately threatened when overtaken by golf's dreaded disease – the twitch, the yips.

Bernhard won that battle, assisted by often putting with his left hand below his right, and his 1980 Dunlop Masters victory sparked a successful career likely to be punctuated with regular major championship triumphs. He is a marvellous driver of the ball and his razor-sharp accuracy with long irons often sets-up rounds such as his marvellous 62 at El Saler during his Spanish Open win in 1984 which secured him number one spot in the European Order of Merit for the second time in four years.

SANDY LYLE
Born: February 9, 1958, Shrewsbury, Shropshire, England.
Lives: Wentworth, Surrey, England.
Height: 6-1. Weight: 187.
Turned Pro: 1977.

Career Highlights
Ryder Cup: 1979, 1981, 1983, 1985.
British Open: 1985.
World Cup: 1979, 1980.
World Cup Individual Winner: 1980.
Nigerian Open: 1978.
Jersey Open: 1979.
Scandinavian Open: 1979.
European Open: 1979.
Coral Classic: 1980.
French Open: 1981.
Lawrence Batley International: 1981, 1982.
Madrid Open: 1983.
Italian Open: 1984.
Lancome Trophy: 1984.
Hennessy Cognac Cup (Individual): 1984.
Kapalua International (Hawaii): 1984.
Casio World Open (Japan): 1984.
Benson and Hedges International: 1985.

Sandy Lyle's road to Open Championship glory in 1985 began when his father, Alex, travelled south from Glasgow to take up a professional-cum-greenskeeper post at the Hawkstone Country Club in Shropshire. It was there – at Shrewsury to be precise – that Sandy was born and there that, at the age of three, he hit his first shot 80 yards with a long-shafted wood while wearing a pair of Wellingtons.

His progress after that was dramatic. He played, during the school holidays, three rounds each day and, at the age of nine, put in his first recorded score of 124. By the age of ten he had broken 80. He enjoyed an excellent amateur career, although he did fail to get a point in the Walker Cup at Shinnecock Hills in New York, but he never had any great desire to turn professional. He went to the PGA European Tour school in 1977 for want of a new goal. And he won the £300 prize with rounds of 75, 73, 73 and 74 at Foxhills Golf and Country Club.

Lyle has carried on winning from then. He immediately came out in 1978 to win the Nigerian Open – starting off with rounds of 61 and 63 on the Ikoyi course in Lagos. Three victories on the European tour followed in 1979 and he has never looked back. There was a minor question-mark when his prodigious driving and marvellous touch failed to blend into success in the States, where he was overshadowed by the efforts of Nick Faldo.

But his appetite for success, which so often appeared to be too easily fulfilled, appeared to be whetted when, at the end of 1984, he embarked on an amazing run of success in which he won the Lancome Trophy, the Kapaulua International in Hawaii and the Casio World Open in Japan – taking his winnings for the year to £300,000. Victory in the Open ensured further wealth and glory . . . but he has not allowed success to go to his head. He remains one of the game's most amiable golfers.

MANUEL PINERO
Born: September 1, 1952, Badajoz, Spain.
Lives: Madrid, Spain.
Height: 5-7. Weight: 143.
Turned Pro: 1968.

Career Highlights
Ryder Cup: 1981, 1985.
World Cup: 1974, 1976 (winner
  with Severiano Ballesteros),
  1979, 1980, 1982 (winner with
  Jose-Maria Canizares), 1983.
World Cup Individual Winner:
1982.
Madrid Open: 1974, 1981, 1985.
Swiss Open: 1976, 1981.
PGA Championship: 1977.
English Classic: 1980.
European Open: 1982.
Italian Open: 1985.

Manuel Pinero's rags-to-riches story began in a small hacienda on a farm near the Spanish-Portuguese border town of Badajoz. When Manuel was born his father, a foreman of a farm where there were 1,000 pigs to look after, was earning the princely sum of 18 pesetas. Mr Pinero, who watched his son every inch of the way at The Belfry, later tried his own business but he was badly let down by a working colleague and, pesetaless, he was compelled to move the family to Madrid to look for work.

Manuel, then 11, immediately became involved in golf simply because the family needed money. He went to caddie at the nearby Club de Campo course. Eventually he joined the caddie school there – it operated between nine and one and three and seven each day, except Sunday, and each of the 75 caddies would sit in the classroom where they could be educated in between requests from the caddie-master for them to "go to work."

Thus Pinero grew up alongside the likes of Jose-Maria Canizares and Antonio Garrido. And, after hitting his first shots with a piece of metal bent into a shape of a club, he progressed into one of Spain's finest golfers. His victory in the 1974 Spanish PGA Championship was a confidence booster but his breakthrough came later that year when he pipped Valentin Barrios in a play-off for the Madrid Open on the full European tour.

There have been many important wins since then – although the money has not changed Pinero as he is still one of the most unassuming guys in the game – but it was the glory that he brought to Spain in 1976 when, with Sevvy Ballesteros, they won the World Cup that meant more to him. "I remember Sevvy crying when I holed a putt at the last for us to win," recalls Manuel. The Ballesteros-Pinero "team" worked a treat again in the Ryder Cup when Jacklin brought them together at the eleventh hour.

JOSE RIVERO
Born: September 20, 1955, Madrid, Spain.
Lives: Madrid, Spain.
Height: 5-10½. Weight: 168.
Turned Pro: 1973.

Career Highlights
Ryder Cup: 1985.
World Cup: 1984 (winner with Jose-Maria Canizares)
Lawrence Batley International: 1984.

When the Spanish Federation pushed £2,000 into Jose Rivero's hand and told him to go and play the tour they could hardly have realised what a change it would make to his livelihood. Rivero, until 1983 a teaching professional with no real desire to follow compatriots like Sevvy Ballesteros and Manuel Pinero onto the tour, accepted the offer made on condition that he paid back half the money even if he failed to win a single peseta.

Rivero soon paid the money back. In 1983 he earned £9,673 in official money, then in 1984, with the help of his first tour win in the Lawrence Batley International, his European winnings multiplied to an amazing £60,861. He earned another £24,000 by teaming-up with Jose-Maria Canizares as Spain won the World Cup in Rome.

Meanwhile Tony Jacklin was becoming increasingly impressed with Rivero. He liked the way that the Spaniard had calmly coaxed home a putt of ten feet on the last green to win the Lawrence Batley International at The Belfry. And he decided that Rivero at The Belfry in the Ryder Cup would be good for Europe. It was a controversial choice but Jacklin insisted: "You need bottle to hole winning putts in the Ryder Cup and Jose proved to me he had it with that ten footer in the Batley."

Rivero, who started as a caddie at Puerta de Hierro in Madrid, became one of ten teaching professionals at La Moraleja, also on the outskirts of Spain's capital, working under the guidance of Valentin Barrios. Rivero had come from a family of nine boys and three girls – his father was often out of work – so life as a teaching professional brought him a better life. The riches of the tour have sweetened it.

SAM TORRANCE
Born: August 24, 1953, Largs, Scotland.
Lives: Largs.
Height: 5-11. Weight: 189.
Turned Pro: 1970.

Career Highlights
Ryder Cup: 1981, 1983, 1985,
World Cup: 1976, 1978, 1982, 1984.
Under-25's Match Play Champion:
    1972.
Radici Open (Italy): 1982.
Zambian Open: 1975.
Piccadilly Medal: 1976.
Martini International: 1976.
Colombian Open: 1979.

Australian PGA 1980.
Carrolls Irish Open: 1981.
Spanish Open: 1982.
Portuguese Open: 1982, 1983.
Scandinavian Open: 1983.
Tunisian Open: 1984.
Benson and Hedges International:
    1984.
Sanyo Open: 1984.
Monte Carlo Open: 1985.

The paradox of Sam Torrance is that he appeared to start climbing golfing Everests after going "Down Under." In his early years on the tour there was much to admire about Torrance as he steadily made progress so that in 1976 he had the game, and the confidence, to win two tour titles in the space of five weeks.

Then came a lull in his achievements and for some years it seemed as if Torrance might not gain from the game everything that was expected from one so talented.

Torrance, however, changed gear when he went to Australia in 1980. He won the PGA Championship and it seemed to galvanise him into wanting to become internationally accepted as one of the world's leading golfers. There was no reason for him not to reach such a target because few golfers were prepared to put in so many hours on the practice range.

In truth Torrance has always found practicing enjoyable simply because most of the time he is hitting shots under the watchful eye of his father, Bob, who is the professional at Largs. Torrance honed his game on the wind blown courses of west Scotland and he is regarded as one of the best manufacturers of shots in the business.

His record breaking year in 1984 – he won a personal best £112,000 in official money for second place in the Order of Merit – confirmed his climb to the top. And for Torrance, arms raised aloft, nothing could match that euphoric moment at The Belfry when his putt toppled into the hole to seal Ryder Cup glory for Europe.

PAUL WAY
Born: March 12, 1963, Kingsbury, Middlesex, England.
Lives: Tunbridge Wells, Kent.
Height: 5-8. Weight: 154.
Turned Pro: 1981.

Career Highlights
Ryder Cup: 1983. 1985.
Walker Cup: 1981.
Dutch Open: 1982.

South African Charity Classic:
1985.
Whyte and Mackay PGA
Championship: 1985.

Tony Jacklin never had any doubts. "He is the finest young prospect this country has," declared Jacklin. And with those words he pitched Paul Way into the Ryder Cup deep end – by pairing him with Severiano Ballesteros in Florida in 1983.

Yet Way's elevation to stardom via the Ryder Cup, was predictable from his teenage days when he played truant from school and made his way from his Kent home to Sunningdale where he would practice his golf often with schoolboy chum Mike McLean, who subsequently joined Way in the professional world.

Dennis Way started his son in the game. And Roy Howard, the headmaster at Hugh Christie School, where Way went, was also a keen sportsman. So he encouraged Way's golfing talent and the youngster, with McLean, won the 1981 Aer Lingus National Championship for the school. Way, who started golf at the age of 11, was down to a six handicap three years later and he was in the Walker Cup team by 1981.

That gave a true indication of his future in the game. And his arrival in the professional ranks was astonishing. He put together a superb last round 65 to take the 1982 Dutch Open. In 1983 there were no wins, but three and a half points out of five in the Ryder Cup, and it was the manner in which he elbowed his way into the side that mostly impressed Jacklin.

The Tournament Players Championship that year represented Way's last chance of winning a place. His desire to succeed spilled over when a rare error led to him banging his one iron on the ground at the 11th and putting it out of commission. It released the tension and Way grabbed his Ryder Cup chance by finishing second. Jacklin immediately predicted: "He'll be a hit from the start!"

Way's 1985 started with a return to the winner's circle in the South African Charity Classic then a sensational play-off win over Sandy Lyle in the Whyte and Mackay PGA Championship at Wentworth.

IAN WOOSNAM
Born: March 2, 1958, Oswestry, Wales.
Lives: Oswestry.
Height: 5-4½. Weight: 147.
Turned Pro: 1976.

Career Highlights
Ryder Cup: 1983, 1985.
World Cup: 1980, 1982, 1983, 1984.
Under-23's Match Play Champion:
   1979.

Under-25's Champion: 1982.
Swiss Open: 1982.
Silk Cut Masters: 1983.
Scandinavian Open: 1984.
Zambian Open: 1985.

Ian Woosnam's star began its ascendancy when he was standing on the practice ground before the start of the 1982 Nigerian Open. Six years as a professional had brought Woosnam nothing but anxiety and apprehension. The trouble was that he never produced his best in the company of good players because he was worried about making a fool of himself. But in Nigeria he took a look at those professionals who were practicing alongside him and suddenly realised that he had to adopt an aggressive attitude on the course in order to turn his career around.

The transformation in 1982 was almost unbelievable. Woosnam, 104th in the Order of Merit in 1981, climbed to eighth place in Europe the following season. Australian Greg Norman, after an exciting head to head duel with Woosnam in the Benson and Hedges International that season, declared: "This guy can beat anybody in Europe. He's a real tiger . . . a great player." Less than one month later Woosnam did beat everybody – he won the Swiss Open – and he has never looked back.

Woosnam learned his golf on the local Llanymynech course, near his father's farm, where 15 of the holes are in Wales and three in England. Even though his home was on the borders there is no doubt about Woosnam being Welsh through and through and his earliest golfing heroes were Brian Huggett and Dai Rees.

Yet there is much to compare Woosnam with the South African genius Gary Player. It is not simply that they are similar in stature: Woosnam possesses that same never-say-die outlook. He is prepared to gamble at anytime, if something can be gained, and he emphasised his attacking qualities during the 1985 Benson and Hedges International at York when he equalled a world record with eight successive birdies in the same round.

4 *US Team: Who's Who*

by Mitchell Platts

RAY FLOYD
Born: September 4, 1942, Fort Bragg, California, U.S.A.
Lives: Miami, Florida.
Height: 6-1. Weight: 200.
Turned Pro: 1961.

Career Highlights

Ryder Cup: 1969, 1975, 1977, 1981, 1983, 1985.
U.S. Masters: 1976.
U.S. PGA: 1969, 1982.
Million Dollar Sun City Challenge: 1982.
St. Petersburg Open: 1963.
St. Paul Open: 1965.
Jacksonville Open: 1969.
American Golf Classic: 1969.
Kemper Open: 1975.
World Open: 1976.
Byron Nelson Classic: 1977.
Pleasant Valley Classic: 1977.
Greensboro Open: 1979.
Doral-Eastern Open: 1980, 1981.
Tournament Players Championship: 1981.
Manufacturers Hanover-Westchester Classic: 1981.
Memorial Tournament: 1982.
Danny Thomas-Memphis Classic: 1982.
Houston Open: 1985.

Ray Floyd is now one of the elder statesmen of the US tour. It was back in 1963, when he won the St. Petersburg Open, that he was chosen Rookie-of-the-Year. Victory came only three years after he had decided on a career in golf rather than one in baseball.

Floyd would be the first to agree that his rise was less than meteoric. He did win the US PGA Championship in 1969 but, mostly, he played a supporting role for his first dozen years on the tour.

What transformed Floyd was marriage. He had – he stresses unfairly – gained a playboy image but with Maria, his wife, at his side, Floyd became a dedicated family man determined to give nothing but his best on the course.

The big breakthrough came, three years after their marriage, in 1976. Floyd opened with rounds of 65 and 66 in the US Masters, virtually ending the championship on Friday night, and he fizzed home an eight shot winner. He now became a regular winner, taking at least one title each year through to 1982 when he captured the US PGA Championship again.

Thus the highlight, as far as Floyd is concerned, of his career is its longevity. He insists that he has played the best golf of his life during the last few years although there is no doubt that an experiment with lightweight clubs in 1984 contributed to an unpredictable down swing in fortune. He sagged to 68th in the money list but once reunited with conventional clubs he returned to winning form in the 1985 Houston Open.

He also retains a passion for the game and, especially, for the Ryder Cup. "The ultimate is to represent your country," said Floyd. "I like the camaraderie the Ryder Cup breeds. It is the one time when the players are actually pulling for each other. It's something we see far too rarely in golf. It's fantastic to have 12 guys in one team bringing that kind of warmth into a match."

HUBERT GREEN
Born: December 28, 1946, Birmingham, Alabama, U.S.A.
Lives: Bay Point, Florida.
Height: 6-1. Weight: 175.
Turned Pro: 1970.

Career Highlights
Ryder Cup: 1977, 1979, 1985.
U.S. Open: 1977.
U.S. PGA: 1985.
Dunlop Pheonix (Japan): 1975.
Carrolls Irish Open: 1977.
Houston Open: 1971.
Tallahassee Open: 1973.
B.C. Open: 1973

Bob Hope Classic: 1974.
Greater Jacksonville Open: 1974, 1976.
Philadelphia Open: 1974.
Walt Disney World National Team Play (with Mac McLendon): 1974
Southern Open: 1975, 1984.
Doral-Eastern Open: 1976.

Sea Pines Heritage Classic: 1976 1978.
Hawaiian Open: 1978, 1979.

New Orleans Open: 1979.
Sammy Davis Jnr-Greater Hartford Open: 1981.

Hubert Green completed a marvellous comeback when he moved past Lee Trevino, the defending champion, to win the US PGA Championship at Cherry Hills. It also earned for him a place in the 1985 US Ryder Cup team.

Green had played in the 1977 and 1979 Ryder Cups but his form in the 1980s, compared with that in the 1970s, led to many observers dismissing his prospects of ever winning a major championship again.

In fact Green had won his previous 'major' – the US Open in 1977 – when he was at the height of his career. He scored 16 victories between coming on the tour in 1971 and 1979. He was Rookie of the Year in 1971 and he also won tournaments in Ireland and Japan.

But, having stayed among the top 15 in the money list for seven successive years, his form tapered off and he spiralled to 135th in the charts in 1983. So victory in the US PGA Championship represented a dramatic U-turn in his fortunes.

Green first swung a club aged five. His father, a sports 'nut', encouraged his son to participate in all pastimes but Hubert gradually eliminated one after another until he was left concentrating on golf. He competed regularly in special invitational events throughout his native Alabama before moving on to Florida State University. He turned professional in 1970 and worked for a summer as an assistant professional at Merion Golf Club before qualifying later that year to play on the tour.

PETER JACOBSEN
Born: March 4, 1954, Portland, Oregon, U.S.A.
Lives: Portland, Oregon.
Height: 6-3. Weight: 190.
Turned Pro: 1976.

Career Highlights
Ryder Cup: 1985
Western Australian Open: 1979.
Johnnie Walker Cup
    (Madrid, Spain): 1981, 1982.

Buick-Goodwrench Open: 1980.
Colonial National Invitation: 1984.
Sammy Davis Jnr-Greater Hartford Open: 1984.

Time was when Peter Jacobsen, one of the most personable players on the US Tour, did not appear to know his own potential. In fact it was not until he won twice in 1984 that he seemed to realise his fine ability. And it is by winning tournaments that Jacobsen aims to be remembered.

He says: "Back in Ben Hogan's day everything was measured by how many you won not how much. Today, of course, with so much cash on the golfing table, success, for the most part, is judged by monetary gains. I want to be judged by what I win. I don't want to be consoled with a fat cheque for finishing fifth or sixth."

Jacobsen has had to be patient waiting to reach such a stage. He first played at the age of 12, learning from his father, who taught him the fundamentals, and his brother, David. He qualified for the US Tour, via the 1976 winter school, but struggled until he won the Buick-Goodwrench Open in 1980.

That victory, coming as it did following an operation on his vocal cords and a period out of the game because of a back injury, provided Jacobsen with increasing confidence. His victories in the 1981 and 1982 Johnnie Walker Trophy in Madrid were important stepping-stones with regard to international recognition.

He has also gained a reputation as a natural mimic. His impersonations of his fellow pro's swings and mannerisms are extremely funny and there are those who claim that if he does ever stop playing golf then he could be just as successful in show-business.

TOM KITE
Born: December 9, 1949, McKinney, Texas, U.S.A.
Lives: Austin, Texas.
Height: 5-8½. Weight: 155.
Turned Pro: 1972.

Career Highlights
Ryder Cup: 1979, 1981, 1983, 1985.
Walker Cup: 1971.
European Open: 1980.
IVB-Bicentennial Golf Classic: 1976.
B.C. Open: 1978.
American Motors-Inverrary
Classic: 1981.
Bay Hill Classic: 1982.
Bing Crosby National Pro-Am: 1983.
Doral-Eastern Open: 1984.
Georgia-Pacific Atlanta Classic: 1984.
Tournament of Champions: 1985.

Tom Kite has won only eight tournaments since he joined the US Tour in 1972. But he has won more than $2.5 million in that time.

Those statistics speak volumes for his style of play. There are few more consistent golfers in the world.

In fact his performance in 1981 mirrors his reputation. He won the inaugural Arnold Palmer PGA Tour award as the leading money winner. He captured the Vardon Trophy for his stroke average of 69.80. And he compiled an incredible 21 top ten finishes in 26 starts. No wonder that the Golf Writers of America named Kite the Player of the Year.

Even so Kite's consistency has strangely deserted him in times of need. Winning a major championship has proved elusive to him – the 1984 US Masters and the 1985 Open Championship both escaping his grasp when the chance of a glorious win presented itself.

At Augusta Kite was locked in an enthralling contest with fellow Texan Ben Crenshaw. But Kite's hopes evaporated at the short 12th where he knocked his tee shot into the water. At Royal St George's, little more than one year later, Kite must have really fancied his chances when he moved clear in the Open with nine holes to play. But no sooner had he established an advantage than he fell back by taking a double bogey at the tenth.

Kite took his first swipe at a golf ball when his father put a club in his hand at the age of six. He gained his first victory at the age of 11 when he won an age-group event at the Country Club of Austin, Texas. Three years later he started to take the game seriously and, after finishing runner-up to Lanny Wadkins in the US Amateur, he was chosen for the Walker Cup team before moving on to the professional pastures.

ANDY NORTH

Born: March 9, 1950, Thorp, Wisconsin, U.S.A.
Lives: Madison, Wisconsin.
Height: 6-4. Weight: 200.
Turned Pro: 1972.

Career Highlights U.S. Open: 1978, 1985.
Ryder Cup: 1985. Westchester Classic: 1977.

"Thank heavens it's over!" That was Andy North's first comment after he won the 1978 US Open Championship at Cherry Hills. And it was hardly surprising that he should breath such a huge sigh of relief. North had won only once before in six years on the tour – the Westchester Classic the previous year. There had been near misses, and cruel disappointments, but he was better known for one dazzling scoring spree than as a title contender. In 1975, at Endicott, New York, North had taken a seven under par 27 on the back nine to lead the BC Open with an first round 63. It put the lanky North's name in the record books as Mike Souchak, in the 1955 Texas Open, was at that time the only person to have scored as low.

North, however, came out and won the 1978 US Open. He reached the last required a bogey five for an outright victory and he made it . . . just! He was in a bunker for three but he splashed out to four feet and, after twice backing away from the putt, coaxed the ball home.

What turned North into an instant TV star was the manner in which he accepted the situation. When he put his third shot into that bunker he simply shrugged his shoulders and smiled. He knew, through regularly practicing with Tom Watson, that this was the test. And that to survive he would need to accept the situation. "I couldn't play that third shot again," he said later. "I had to think positively – of getting up and down in two."

Victory should have provided the impetus for further success. Instead, he went backwards. Injury had introduced North to the game; now injury threatened to end his career. At school North played only basketball and football – until it was discovered that a bone in his knee had stopped growing and was disintegrating. It was so serious that he spent 18 months on crutches before being told that the one game he could play was golf as he could ride in a cart. He became a star at the University of Florida, where he was chosen All-American in golf for three years. The knee healed, assisted by corrective surgery, but in the early 1980s another problem developed – initially thought to be tendonitis of the right elbow.

North was in constant discomfort. An examination revealed a bone spur and further surgery in late 1983 eliminated the problem and the pain. North, however, was by now swinging inconsistently, bad habits had crept in as he continued to play through a personal pain barrier, and in 1984 he slipped to 149th in the Official Money List as he struggled to get his act together.

But he had the star role again in the 1985 US Open at Oakland Hills, Michigan, where a marvellous bunker shot at the penultimate hole enabled him to seize the initiative as a handful of contenders fell away. Only 15 of the 61 golfers who have won the US Open have managed to accomplish the feat more than once. Arnold Palmer, Gary Player and Tom Watson have had to settle for one win each – North may have won only three events in his career but at least two of them have been US Opens.

MARK O'MEARA

Born: January 13, 1957, Goldsboro, North Carolina, U.S.A.
Lives: Palm Desert, California.
Height: 6-0. Weight: 175.
Turned Pro: 1980.

Career Highlights
Ryder Cup: 1985.
Greater Milwaukee Open: 1984.

Bing Crosby National Pro-Am: 1985.
Hawaiian Open: 1985.

In 1984 Mark O'Meara changed from being relatively unknown to a household name. He joined the tour in 1981, and he finished as low as 118th in the 1982 Official Money List, but in 1984 he rocketed to second place with $465,873. He won only once, the Greater Milwaukee Open, but he finished second on five occasions, third three times and he had no fewer than 15 top ten finishes.

The confidence derived from those performances enabled him to come out and win the Bing Crosby and Hawaiian Open tournaments, back to back, in 1985. He earned an astonishing $180,000 for those two weeks' work.

In reality, however, it has taken O'Meara an enormous amount of work to climb to the top. He turned professional after winning the US Amateur in 1979 but he soon discovered that he needed help. He turned to Hank Haney, a teaching professional from Houston, Texas. And he went about rebuilding his swing – working on the Ben Hogan theory of being "be a little flatter going down."

O'Meara accepted that he could not copy Hogan. But he was convinced that he could adapt the principles that Hogan used. Haney, who had studied many films of Hogan, stood by all the time as O'Meara worked on refining his own swing. It took two years but the value of such an investment is now reflected by his standing on the tour.

O'Meara started to play the game at the age of 13 after his family moved to Mission Viejo, California. Being new to the neighbourhood, the young O'Meara knew few people so during his out-of-school hours he would slip onto the nearby golf course. O'Meara fell head over heels in love with the game from the start . . . and he has never stopped strengthening the relationship.

CALVIN PEETE
Born: July 18, 1943, Detroit, Michigan, U.S.A.
Lives: Fort Myers, Florida.
Height: 5-10. Weight: 165.
Turned Pro: 1971.

Career Highlights
Ryder Cup: 1983, 1985.
Greater Milwaukee Open: 1979, 1982.
Anheuser-Busch Classic: 1982, 1983.
B.C. Open: 1982.
Pensacola Open: 1982.
Georgia-Pacific Atlanta Classic: 1983.
Texas Open: 1984.
Phoenix Open: 1985.
Tournament Players Championship: 1985.

Since he won the Greater Milwaukee Open in 1979 the Calvin Peete story has been well documented.

It is the story of a black boy born to struggle on the streets of Detroit. He then moved south to a Florida farm where he lived with his 18 brothers and sisters – through two marriages by his father. There, forced to drop out of school at an early age to assist the family expenses, he worked picking beans and corn before moving into the business of selling goods to migrant farm workers.

Peete packed clothes, rings, watches and anything else he could squeeze into his station wagon. He followed the field hands, who had not the time to visit the big city stores. And he travelled the east coast from Florida north to Rochester, New York.

In Rochester Peete had friends who played golf. He was invited to play. Time and time again he turned them down. "I couldn't see any sense in chasing a little ball around under a hot sun," he recalls. But, at the age of 23, he finally agreed. It was 1966 and he had read how Jack Nicklaus was making $200,000 each year chasing the ball. It was time to play.

Even so, to succeed Peete has had to disprove golf's straight left arm theory. As a youth he suffered a broken left elbow, falling from an apple tree, and he still cannot fully extend his left arm. In fact in 1983 he won the Golf Writers' Ben Hogan award which is annually given to the individual who had to overcome a physical handicap or illness to play the game.

Peete, of course, has overcome much more than that. And in doing so he has achieved success in the game the like of which must have been a dream. When he won the Tournament Players Championship in 1985 it was his tenth US tour win in seven years and it took his official earnings past the $1.5m mark.

CRAIG STADLER
Born: June 2, 1953, San Diego, California, U.S.A.
Lives: Reno, Nevada.
Height: 5-10. Weight: 200.
Turned Pro: 1975.

Career Highlights
Ryder Cup: 1983, 1985.
U.S. Masters: 1982.
Walker Cup: 1975.
European Masters: 1985.
Bob Hope Desert Classic: 1980.

Greater Greensboro Open: 1980.
Kemper Open: 1981, 1982.
Joe Garagiola-Tucson Open: 1982.
Kemper Open: 1982.
World Series of Golf: 1982.
Byron Nelson Classic: 1984.

Most internationally respected golfers can look back on their career and select one year when they established themselves. For chunky Craig Stadler "The Walrus" that year was 1982 – he won four tournaments including the US Masters.

Stadler had first played golf at the age of five. He began to take it seriously three or four years later, then won such titles as the World Junior Championship, the San Diego City Amateur and the Southern California Interscholastic. He proved himself an expert putter as he coaxed the ball time and time again into the cup on the way to winning the 1973 US Amateur Championship – graduating to Walker Cup honours two years later before turning professional.

But Stadler's first attempt to join the tour was a failure. He had to try a second time, in the Spring of 1976, before receiving his players' card although it was not until 1980 that he won for the first time.

Stadler's two successes that year, followed by another in the Kemper Open in 1981, gave him the confidence to come out in 1982 and play with more aggression. He has gained a reputation for throwing a club or two in frustration but he held himself together well at Augusta to win a play-off with Dan Pohl.

By the end of 1982 Stadler had won $446, 462, easily sufficient for him to be number one in the money list, but he slid back to 17th the following year before climbing to eighth in 1984, when he won the Byron Nelson Classic with the help of a superb seven under par third round of 64. In 1985 he improved his international standing by winning the Ebel European Masters at Crans-sur-Sierre . . . although one week later his pride was dented when he missed that "tiddler" on the second day of the Ryder Cup which transformed morale in both camps.

CURTIS STRANGE
Born: January 30, 1955, Norfolk, Virginia, U.S.A.
Lives: Kingsmill, Virginia.
Height: 5-11. Weight: 170.
Turned Pro: 1976.

Career Highlights
Ryder Cup: 1983, 1985.
Walker Cup: 1975.
Pensacola Open: 1979.
Michelob-Houston Open: 1980.
Manufacturers Hanover
   Westchester Classic: 1980.

Sammy Davis Jnr-Greater
   Hartford Open: 1983.
LaJet Classic: 1984.
Honda Classic: 1985.
Panasonic Las Vegas
   International: 1985.
Canadian Open: 1985.

Curtis Strange will forever look back on the year of 1985 with mixed feelings. It was, without question, the year in which he demonstrated to the golfing world his immense ability. He captured no fewer than three tournaments, including the Canadian Open, and he established a new money record by surpassing the previous best of 530,808 dollars set by Tom Watson in 1980.

Strange, however, allowed the chance of golfing immortality to slip when he failed to put his name alongside those "greats" who have won the prestigious U.S. Masters. Instead he was consigned to what must have seemed a lifetime of explanations when he took sixes at the 13th and 15th holes at Augusta and thereby opened the door for Bernhard Langer to win.

Strange's father was a golf professional who owned the White Sands Country Club in Virginia Beach, Virginia, and it was there, at the age of seven, that Curtis struck his first shots. Within one year he was playing every day and a career in the game was being forged. He enjoyed a brilliant time as an amateur which included being named the 1974 College Player of the Year then earning his place on the 1975 Walker Cup team.

Then, as an amateur, he had his first brush with the U.S. Masters – finishing remarkably in a tie for 15th place. That was in April of 1976 and, later that year, he turned professional.

From the moment that he gained his professional breakthrough, winning the Pensacola Open in 1979, he became recognised as one of the most determined and talented players in the game. The key to him becoming a multi-winner in 1985 was in his own ability to use more patience and control his emotions.

HAL SUTTON
Born: April 28, 1958, Shreveport, Lousiana, U.S.A.
Height: 6-1. Weight: 185.
Turned Pro: 1981.

Career Highlights
Ryder Cup: 1985.
U.S. PGA Championship: 1983.
U.S. Amateur Champion: 1980.
Walt Disney World Golf Classic:
1982.
Tournament Players Championship:
1983.
Memphis Classic: 1985.
LaJet Classic: 1985.

Hal Sutton was not enamoured of the spectators during the Ryder Cup but he was impressed by the manner in which Bernhard Langer beat him five and four. What impressed Sutton most was that Langer could perform so well with a grip that was clearly unorthodox.

When Sutton burst onto the professional scene, winning the Walt Disney World Golf Classic as a rookie then taking the U.S. PGA Championship and the Tournament Players' Championship in only his second season, he still had his critics. Some experts told him that his grip was too strong and that his swing would not stand the test of time.

"I was stupid enough to listen," says Sutton. "I watched Bernhard and I realised that I had wasted 18 months. My grip, even at its strongest, is not as strong as his. I knew then that there is nothing wrong with a strong grip."

Sutton left The Belfry determined to return to the grip which made him leading money winner and PGA Player of the Year in 1983. He went straight into action in the Southwest Golf Classic at Fairway Oaks, Abilene, Texas, and there defied a 40 mph wind to beat Mike Reid at the first hole of a sudden death play-off.

It provided the icing on the cake of a comeback season for Sutton – following a 1984 in which his desire waned to the point that he found himself simply going through the motions so that there was no chance of him reaching what were only half-hearted targets.

The trouble, of course, was that Sutton needed to set himself high goals following his astonishing arrival in the game. Initially it seemed that he might remain an amateur. His father, an oil millionaire, offered him a place in the company but that convinced Sutton he would need to turn professional because he found himself going as long as a month without playing.

So Sutton, who had won the U.S. Amateur in 1980, came out to play for pay. He soon impressed his new colleagues and rivals –

including Jack Nicklaus. "He will win many, many more championships and he will win many major championships," said Nicklaus, after being pipped by Sutton for the U.S. PGA title.

Sutton had already proved himself with eight top ten finishes in his 1982 rookie campaign – winning the Walt Disney World Golf Classic in the final event of the season with a birdie at the fourth extra hole against Bill Britton. Victory took his earnings that season to $237,434. He climbed to number one in the cash charts in 1983, slipped to 26th in 1984 but he recovered in style in 1985 . . . with a little bit of help from Bernhard Langer and the Ryder Cup!

LEE TREVINO (Non-Playing Captain)
Born: December 1, 1939, Dallas, Texas, U.S.A.
Lives: Dallas, Texas.
Height: 5-7. Weight: 180.
Turned Pro: 1960.

Career Highlights
Ryder Cup: 1969, 1971, 1973, 1975, 1979, 1981.
Ryder Cup captain: 1985.
U.S. Open: 1968, 1971.
British Open: 1971, 1972.
U.S. PGA Championship: 1974, 1984.
Benson and Hedges International: 1978.
Lancome Trophy: 1978.
Dunhill Masters: 1985.
Hawaiian Open: 1968.
Tucson Open: 1969, 1970.
National Airlines: 1970.
Tallahassee Open: 1971.

Danny-Thomas Memphis Classic: 1971, 1972, 1980.
Canadian Open: 1971, 1977, 1979.
Sahara: 1971.
Hartford: 1972.
St Louis: 1972.
Jackie Gleason-Inverrary: 1973.
Doral-Eastern: 1973.
New Orleans: 1974.
Florida Citrus Open: 1975.
Colonial National Invitation: 1976.
Tournament Players Championship: 1980.
San Antonio-Texas Open: 1980.
Mony Tournament of Champions: 1981.

They could make a film of Lee Trevino one day. It is a fascinating tale, this story of a chunky young kid, the grandson of a Mexican gravedigger, who never knew his father and lived his formative years in a shack where there was no heating, light or running water. At five he worked in the onion fields; at eight he caddied; at 28 he won his first U.S. Open after only a handful of tour appearances; at 35 he was struck by lightning and should have died; at 44 he was still playing with such brilliance that he won the U.S.

62

PGA Championship at Shoal Creek, Alabama, in a pulsating finish with Gary Player and Lanny Wadkins.

The life and times of Trevino are basically about a poor kid getting rich out of the game. But, more importantly, they are about a man who was prepared to give back to golf. Trevino's asset is that he is fairly dripping in charisma and he has an instant rapport with any person, any fan, who walks down the fairway with him. "Laughing Lee" is a free spirit who has never allowed adversity, like losing a fortune in a real estate development, or the threat of death – when he was raced to hospital in 1975, struggling to breathe, after the lightning attack – to blunt his firm premise: life is fun.

In fact it was not so much fun at The Belfry. Yet Trevino will not worry over defeat simply because he has more knowledge than most Americans of the improvement in European golfing standards. And he says: "I declared, from the start, that I wanted to be the U.S. captain when the Ryder Cup was held in Britain. In America it simply doesn't attract the same interest. Here the people care about the game."

Trevino cares. And he cares about his game. Which is why in 1987, when the Ryder Cup returns to America, he could be involved again . . . as a player. He won the Dunhill Masters at Woburn Golf and Country Club in 1985 – nailing a three wood with that familiar left to right shape with such accuracy that the putt for a winning eagle was a mere formality – to show that age has not blunted his aggressive skill. His career earnings in the United States alone are in excess of $3m – and that sum is likely to swell considerably over the forthcoming years.

LANNY WADKINS
Born: December 5, 1949, Richmond, Virginia, U.S.A.
Lives: Dallas, Texas.
Height: 5-9. Weight: 160.
Turned Pro: 1971.

Career Highlights

Ryder Cup: 1977, 1979, 1983, 1985.
U.S. PGA Championship: 1977.
Walker Cup: 1969, 1971.
U.S. Amateur Champion: 1970.
Bridgestone Open (Japan): 1979.
World Nissan Championship
   (Japan): 1984.

Sahara Invitational: 1972.
Byron Nelson Classic: 1973.
USI Classic: 1973.
World Series of Golf: 1977.
Glen Campbell Los Angeles Open:
   1979, 1985.
Tournament Players Championship:
   1979.

Phoenix Open: 1982.
Mony Tournament of Champions: 1982, 1983.
Buick Open: 1982.
Greater Greesboro Open: 1983.
Bob Hope Classic: 1985.

Lanny Wadkins has a love affair going with the Ryder Cup. It's not surprising. He has won 12 of the 17 matches he has played. He says: "I enjoy the team things even more than our tournaments. You're not just playing for yourself, but for your country and the other guys."

Wadkins, who is proud that he also represented his country in the Walker Cup, emphasised his tenacity in the 1983 Ryder Cup. He regards the wedge shot which he played from 75 yards to "gimmee" distance as one executed under the severest pressure he has ever felt in golf. It earned for Wadkins a half with Jose-Maria Canizares; it rescued the United States from the embarrassment of defeat on their home soil.

In fact Wadkins lost his singles to Manuel Pinero in the 1985 version. But his entire career has been punctuated by such surprises. When he came out of the U.S. Qualifying School in 1971 – incidentally the same one from which Tom Watson emerged – and exploded into action by winning in 1972, the American scene was convinced that a multi-major championship winner had emerged.

Wadkins, however, has picked-up only one of the "Big Four". He won the U.S. PGA Championship in 1977 – edging out the more experienced Gene Littler in a play-off at Pebble Beach. Watson does not have a PGA Championship but he has five British Opens, two U.S. Masters and one U.S. Open.

The roller-coaster existence of Wadkins – he was fifth on the U.S. money list in 1973, down to 88th in 1975, back to third in 1977, down again to 81st in 1981 and up again to third in 1983 – can partly be explained through illness and injury. In 1974 he found it difficult to maintain his energy and he later underwent an operation for a diseased gall bladder to be removed. He now accepts that, against doctor's orders, he returned too early. Bad habits crept into his golf.

Then, after an excellent comeback year in 1977, he suffered from a torn rib muscle, sustained when pulling a suitcase out of the boot of his car, and he went into another slump. That ended, to the astonishment of his rivals, at the Tournament Players Championship at Sawgrass in 1979. He had won, a month earlier in the Los Angeles Open, but his play at the TPC had to be seen to be believed. More than half the field failed to break 300 as gale force winds gusted off the sea, but Wadkins pulled clear to win by five shots from Watson with a five under par 282.

Wadkins knows that he has collected a platoon of critics over the years for throwing clubs in frustration and, on occasions, brushing aside autograph-hunting young fans who happen to catch him at the wrong moment. But Wadkins has won an army of admirers for the aggressive manner he goes about his work. He accepts calculated gambles as part of the game – sensing that a drilled one iron over water can earn an eagle chance and also satisfy the spectators' appetite for excitement.

FUZZY ZOELLER
Born: November 11, 1951, New Albany, Indiana, U.S.A.
Lives: New Albany, Indiana.
Height: 5-10. Weight: 190.
Turned Pro: 1973.

Career Highlights
Ryder Cup: 1979, 1983, 1985.
U.S. Masters: 1979.
U.S. Open: 1984.
Wickes-Andy Williams San Diego
   Open: 1979.

Colonial National Invitation: 1981.
Sea Pines Heritage Classic: 1983.
Las Vegas Pro-Celebrity Classic:
   1983.
Bay Hill Classic: 1985.

It was the most significant gesture of the 1984 sporting year. Fuzzy Zoeller, standing in the middle of the 18th fairway at Winged Foot, took a white towel from his golf bag as ahead of him on the green the Australian Greg Norman holed a monster putt which Zoeller thought was for a birdie. Zoeller waved the towel in mock surrender. He smiled at a time when he thought he had lost. It confirmed golf's enviable reputation as the game for gentlemen.

In fact, as it turned out, Norman's putt was for a par. And Zoeller, by matching it, earned an 18-hole play-off which he won. The play-off, too, unfolded in the most sporting fashion so that Zoeller and Norman, the victor and the vanquished, had done much to enhance the game's enormous respectability.

Zoeller has been doing that much of his life. He is an outstanding ambassador for golf – bringing colour and candour from the moment he blossomed as a superstar by following his first tour win in the 1979 San Diego Open by capturing the U.S. Masters at Augusta a few months later. He came from six shots back to beat Tom Watson and the luckless Ed Sneed in a play-off.

It was the first time, since the inaugural Masters, that a golfer, making his debut at Augusta, had won the prestigious championship. But Zoeller had given an indication of his unpredictable ways when in the 1976 Quad Cities Open, during only his second year on tour, he birdied the last eight holes of the first round to tie Bob Goalby's all-time Tour record established in the 1961 St. Petersburg Open.

Zoeller, however, has made a habit of achieving what would appear to be the impossible. In 1984, a few months after his U.S. Open triumph, he went to the Hospital for Special Surgery in New York. Zoeller, since his high school days when he was injured playing basketball, had suffered from a bad back. The pain, however, was now worse than ever. He was compelled, more and more, to wear a corset at times so that his caddie needed to pick the ball out of the hole. Zoeller needed an operation.

The surgeon chiselled one ruptured disc out from his back and repaired another. There was some fear of him not being able to play again. Yet Zoeller came out in 1985 to win the Bay Hill Classic – pushing Tom Watson into second place. It was, for many, the most pleasing sight of the year.

5 *The Belfry*

illustrated by John James

The Belfry – the setting for the Ryder Cup 1985

Card of The Brabazon Course

Hole	Yards	Par	Hole	Yards	Par
1	418	4	10	275	4
2	349	4	11	420	4
3	465	4	12	235	3
4	579	5	13	394	4
5	399	4	14	194	3
6	396	4	15	550	5
7	183	3	16	410	4
8	460	4	17	575	5
9	400	4	18	474	4
OUT	3649	36	**IN**	3527	36
			OUT	3649	36
			TOTAL	7176	72

The Belfry, nestling just north of Birmingham, is the pride of Midlands golf courses and national headquarters of the European Professional Golfers' Association.

The complex was first envisaged only 15 years ago when the land was mainly used for potato farming. Now two first class courses have been constructed, The Brabazon and The Derby.

The 1985 Ryder Cup was contested over The Brabazon, a beautiful, picturesque course punctuated by lakes and streams.

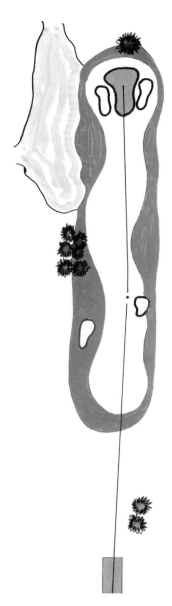

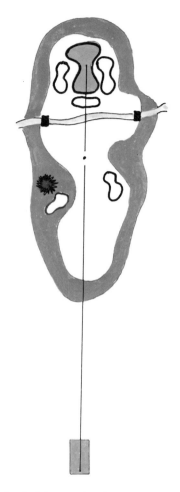

Hole 1: *418 yards. Par 4*
A relatively straightforward start, provided you do not push your tee shot into the right hand bunker. If you drive too far left the bunker to the left of the green makes for a tricky approach.

Hole 2: *349 yards. Par 4*
The stream runs 10 yards short of the green, which is well protected by a phalanx of bunkers. No heroics here. A long iron off the tee and down the narrow fairway short of the stream. Then a wedge in.

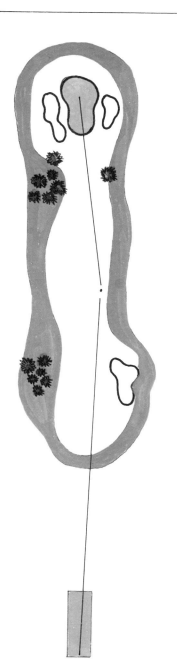

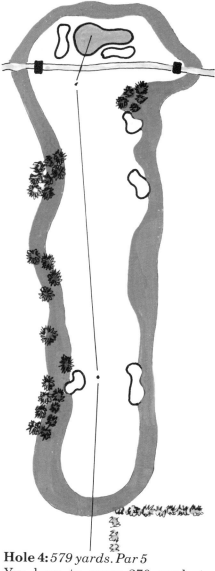

Hole 4: *579 yards. Par 5*
You have to carry 270 yards to reach the 30 yards wide fairway. Then another good wood to lay up short of the stream, preferably on the left side.

Hole 3: *465 yards. Par 4*
The bunker on the right waits at the perfect driving length, some 250 yards from the tee. Even if you miss that it needs another fine blow to find the green on this tough hole.

69

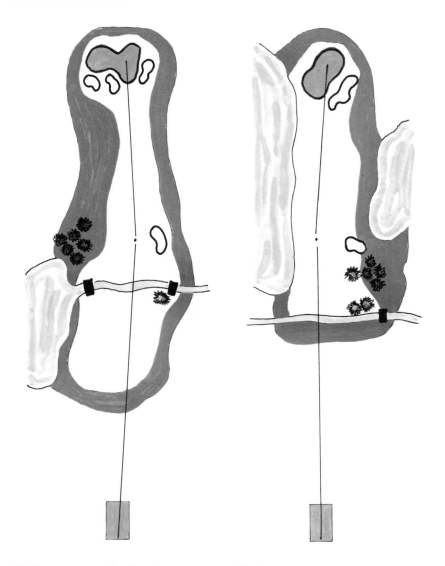

Hole 5: *399 yards. Par 4.*
First comes the stream 200 yards up the fairway, followed by a double-level green festooned with bunkers. Really tricky.

Hole 6: *396 yards. Par 4*
The left of the fairway must be avoided at all costs. It is a lake. But if you fire too far right, the newly positioned fairway bunker will catch you out.

70

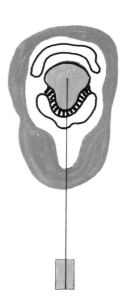

Hole 7: *183 yards. Par 3*

Trees to the right, a rivetted bunker to the front and a huge sand trap behind means that the smallest mistake spells doom. The elevated green truly is an oasis.

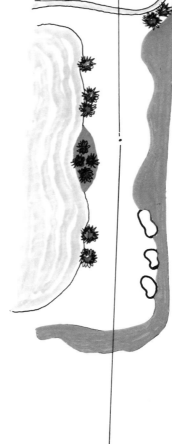

Hole 8: *460 yards. Par 4*

The lake on the left and the line-up of bunkers on the right ensure that only the straightest of drives succeeds. The second shot, a long-iron for the Ryder Cup pros, has to carry the stream and find the well protected green. Very tough.

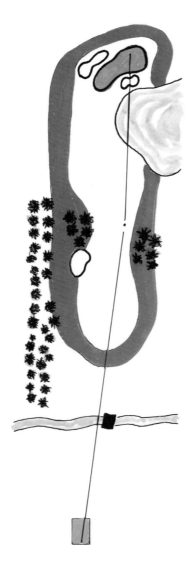

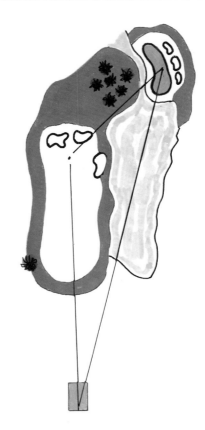

Hole 9: *400 yards. Par 4*
The line on this slight dog-leg left
is to skirt the left-sided bunker to
give maximum sight of the green
for the relatively simple second. A
pin placement to the right and
back of the green brings the lake
into play.

Hole 10: *275 yards. Par 4*
This hole was shortened to
275 yards for the Ryder Cup to provide the tempting alternative of a
drive over the lake. Even when it is
its regulation 300 yards, however,
Sevvy Ballesteros has defied lake,
trees and low-flying aircraft to hit
the green. Trevino ordered his
foursomes to play safe, hitting
mid-irons short of the bunkers and
pitching in. Jacklin allowed his
Europeans to decide for themselves.

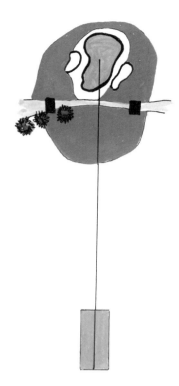

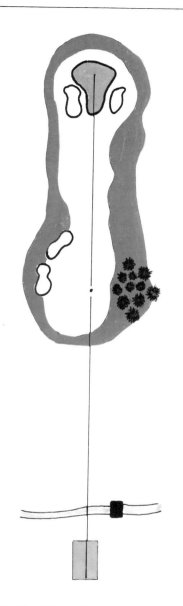

Hole 12: *235 yards. Par 3.*
The upsloping green, bunkered on both sides, is at least a three wood away from the tee. And it is guarded by the meandering stream. Difficult par 3.

Hole 11: *420 yards. Par 4*
Another hole which calls for accurate driving. Two fearsome fairway bunkers wait on the left, a mass of trees on the right. Nor is the approach easy into a narrow green well guarded either side.

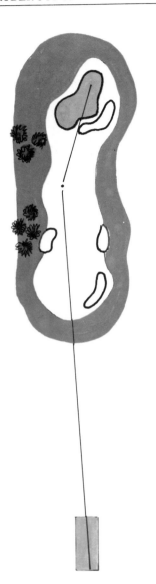

Hole 14: *194 yards. Par 3*
The mounds at the back encourage players to fly the hole rather than run up into the tiered green. The last of the short holes and potentially the easiest.

Hole 13: *394 yards. Par 4*
This hole has been lengthened to bring the right hand bunkers into contention for anything off line. Provided these are negotiated, it needs only a pitch to the green which is protected by a massive bunker.

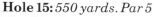

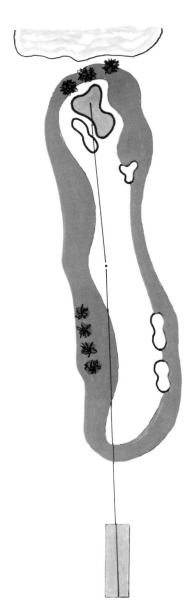

Hole 15: *550 yards. Par 5*
The big hitter going for birdies faces a really difficult second shot here with the green so well protected by bunkers. The less powerful players go to the right of the fairway with their second to open up the three-tiered green for a wedge.

Hole 16: *410 yards. Par 4*
A dog-leg left with a difficult right-to-left tiered green. The front bunker ensures that the target area is small... and this decreases even more when the pin is on the right.

Hole 17: *575 yards. Par 5*
So tempting to try and cut the
corner of this left-to-right dog-leg.
But a clump of forbidding poplar
trees stands in the way close to a
mighty bunker. The reward
is a relatively open
green.

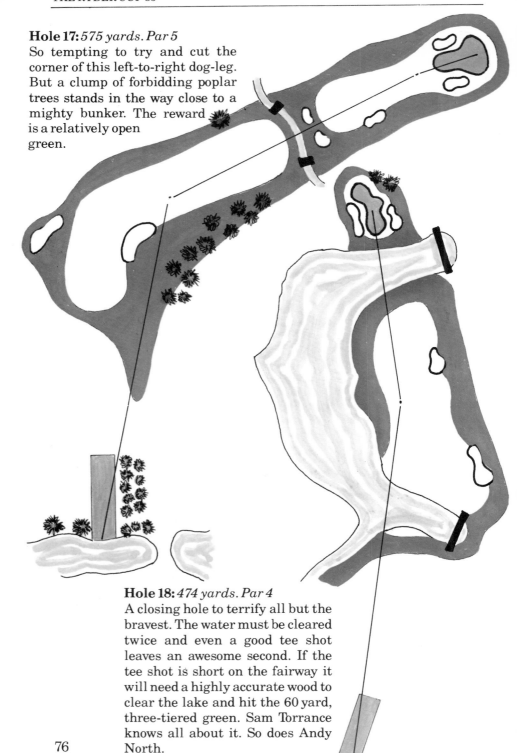

Hole 18: *474 yards. Par 4*
A closing hole to terrify all but the
bravest. The water must be cleared
twice and even a good tee shot
leaves an awesome second. If the
tee shot is short on the fairway it
will need a highly accurate wood to
clear the lake and hit the 60 yard,
three-tiered green. Sam Torrance
knows all about it. So does Andy
North.

6

Match by Match
by Martin Hardy

The Europeans marched towards the battle with their heads high and their chests puffed out following a remarkable piece of pre-match motivation by captain Tony Jacklin.

As the respective flags of the competing nations were raised, along with them went a few eyebrows, for Jacklin proceded to out-hype the Americans in a field where they had previously reigned par excellence.

The two captains were called upon to introduce their teams. American leader Lee Trevino – usually never short of a thousand words or two – was subdued and low key. He called his 12 ambassadors quickly and by name alone, pausing only at Andy North to acknowledge him as U.S. Open champion.

Then up stepped Jacklin, the showman. He detailed the career highlights of all his men – much to the cheering delight of about 3,000 people gathered around the putting green and frontage of The Belfry Hotel.

When he came to Yorkshireman Howard Clark he completed his appraisal by pointing out that Clark had twice beaten the legendary Tom Watson in the Ryder Cup. No-one in the crowd seemed to realise that it had been only once, although his 1981 success was by a crushing four and three.

Sandy Lyle, after his Open triumph, and West Germany's Bernhard Langer, following his magnificent capture of the U.S. Masters title, received particular praise as Jacklin warmed to his theme.

But it was for the last man in his line-up that Jacklin saved his most glowing tribute.

"Sevvy Ballesteros," he said, thumping out the words, "twice Open champion, twice Masters champion and, for me, the best golfer in the world."

The Europeans beamed with pride. If the Americans smiled it was through clenched teeth.

Nobody normally upstages Trevino. Jacklin had . . . and it was with this superb piece of confidence building one-upmanship that the Europeans assembled into battle formation.

FRIDAY FOURSOMES

Ballesteros & Pinero v Strange & O'Meara

1 FRIDAY/FOURSOMES

PLAYERS	1	2	3	4	5	6	7	8	9	OUT	10	11	12	13	14	15	16	17	18	IN	TOTAL
	4	4	4	5	4	4	3	4	4		4	4	3	4	3	5	4	5	4		
BALLESTEROS	A/S	+1	+2		+3	+4	+3	+2	4	36	+3		+4		+3		+2	5	4	3ª	
+ PINERO	4	4	4	4	4	4	4	4	4	36	3	4	3	4	4	4	4	5		NIN 2+1
STRANGE	4	5	5	4	5	5	3	3	4	38	4	4	4	4	3	4	3	5		
O'MEARA																				

Jacklin had intended to partner Ballesteros with fellow country-man and Ryder Cup newcomer Jose Rivero, but changed his mind in the final practice round when Rivero showed erratic form. So it was with Pinero, his little, but lionhearted fellow Spaniard, that Ballesteros set off. Facing them were leading American money-winner Curtis Strange and Mark O'Meara, the 28-year-old from North Carolina, who had finished third at The Open.

It was the Americans' indifferent play rather than any spec-tacular shots from the Spaniards which sent Europe flying into a four hole lead after six.

The Americans bogeyed the par four second when O'Meara put Strange in a greenside bunker and then missed from nine ft. Strange similarly misread the second green when he failed to hole from four ft for another bogey. Both sides birdied the fourth, but the Americans' bogey blues caught up with them again at the par four fifth and sixth holes. O'Meara's hooked tee shot on the fifth and his approach into a bunker on the next left the Europeans needing only pars to win both holes. They succeeded.

Pinero not only missed the green with his tee shot at the 183 yd seventh, but also a five ft putt. The Americans won their first hole with a par and, when Strange holed from 12 ft at the next, the gap had been reduced to only two holes.

No wonder the 10th is officially called "The Ballesteros Hole". A plaque marks the place from where he became the first player ever to drive the green – a monster blow of 300 yards, all carry. Shortened specifically for the Ryder Cup, the 275 yards again proved within range for Ballesteros . . . and the fiercely partisan crowd yelled their appreciation. Pinero propelled the first putt of 90 ft to within five of the hole and Ballesteros did the rest for a winning birdie.

The gap increased to four holes on the 12th when Strange missed the green and O'Meara also failed to find it with his recovery chip. The American waywardness afflicted the Europeans on the 14th with Ballesteros at fault and the gap was just two with as many to play after 16 when Strange's three ft birdie putt claimed the hole.

But the comeback and the match ended on the 17th with a half in fives producing a two and one win for Ballesteros and Pinero.

Jacklin had the start he wanted.

Strange and O'Meara wait to tee off

Langer & Faldo v Peete & Kite

2 FRIDAY / FOURSOMES																				
	4	4	5	4	3	4	4				4	4	3	4	3	5	4	5	4	
PLAYERS	1	2	3	4	5	6	7	8	9	OUT	10	11	12	13	14	15	16	17	18	IN	TOTAL
	4	4	4	3	4	4	3	4	4		4	4	3	4	3	3	4	5	4		
LANGER & FALDO	A/S	4	6	4	4	4	3	3	5	37	5	5	3	4	3	5	4				
PEETE & KITE	4	4	4	4	4	4	2	4	3	33	3	4	4	4	3	5	4			WIN	
			+1				+2	+1	+2			+3	+4	+3							3+2

Langer, the quiet, blond West German, and Nick Faldo – an equally private person with huge natural talent – were paired again following their successful partnership two years earlier in America.

Jacklin was banking on the same chemistry. But this time the formula was a dud.

There would have been little to choose between Langer and Faldo two years ago, but since then a not inconsiderable gap has developed. Langer could claim, but wouldn't, that only Ballesteros holds more right to being world number one. Faldo has slipped down the rankings, spending more time in America and trying to get to grips with the intricacies of a new swing. One of Jacklin's three invitées, his had been an expected but controversial selection.

Against them were Calvin Peete, the most successful black golfer of all time and Tom Kite, arguably the best American never to have won a major tournament.

There were early signs that Faldo's form was still deserting him. When he drove into a bunker on the third, Langer topped the attempted recovery with a three wood and Faldo was still short with a six iron. The Americans' par, against a double bogey, was enough to put them ahead – an advantage the Europeans never reduced.

A 40 ft birdie putt on the short seventh doubled the gap although Langer halved it again with a 10 footer on the next. But Faldo's wayward driver put his team in trouble on the ninth and the Americans turned for home with a two hole advantage.

It was soon three as Langer hit the water at the 10th; and at the next he missed from three feet to go four down. The Americans' only blemish came on the short 12th when Peete bunkered his partner.

Three down and five to play was too much for Faldo and Langer. They were beaten on the 16th green, three and two. The Americans had struck back immediately.

Lyle & Brown v Wadkins & Floyd

3 FRIDAY / FOURSOMES

PLAYERS	1	2	3	4	5	6	7	8	9	OUT	10	11	12	13	14	15	16	17	18	IN	TOTAL
LYLE	A/S	4	4	5	4	4	3	4	4		4	4	3	4	3	5	4	5	4		
& BROWN	4	4	5	5	4	5	4	5	5	41	5	4	3	4	4	4					
WADKINS	4	4	4	5	4	4	4	5	4	38	4	4	3	5	2	4					WIN
& FLOYD		+1			+2			+3			+4			+3	+4						4&3

Lyle had shown fine form following the celebrations at Royal St George's where he succeeded Jacklin as the first home Open winner since 1969. Ken Brown, another of Jacklin's invitées, had had a less spectacular season, preferring to spend as much time as possible in America.

Against them were Lanny Wadkins and Ray Floyd, two of the toughest competitors in the world. They were to prove much too formidable for the Europeans in a most one-sided game. The Americans won at a canter without being tested, or indeed, showing particularly good form.

Lyle and Brown scrambled their way round almost from the off and although they scraped a half at the second their erratic play was punished at the next. They were twice in the rough and Lyle was left with a 25 ft putt for a half which proved beyond him.

It took them four blows to get on the green at the sixth and, not surprisingly, they fell two down. Brown had a chance to pull one back on the seventh, but missed from two ft while Lyle put his partner in water on the ninth. The Americans, although two over par for the front nine, were still three up.

It became four on the 10th when the Europeans got their feet wet again and although the 13th proved a lucky one for them as the Americans bogeyed, it was to be their only success – and immediately negated on the short 14th. A par four on the 15th was enough to produce a four and three victory for Trevino's pair.

Lyle, desperately disappointed with himself, went off to practice alone. He was to take no further part in the day's events, Jacklin dropping both him and Brown for the afternoon fourballs.

Clark & Torrance v Stadler & Sutton

4 FRIDAY / FOURSOMES

PLAYERS	1	2	3	4	5	6	7	8	9	OUT	10	11	12	13	14	15	16	17	18	IN	TOTAL
CLARK	A/S	4	4	A/S	+1	4	3	4	4		A/S	4	A/S	4	3	3	4	5	4		
, TORRANCE	4	4	5	3	4	5	4	5	4	38	3	5	2	5	4	5	4				
STADLER	4	3	5	4	4	6	3	4	4	37	4	4	4	4	3	4	4				WIN
, SUTTON		+1				A/S	+1					+1		+1	+2	+3					3+2

Both Clark and Sam Torrance entered the tournament with excellent credentials and consistent swings. But Craig "The Walrus" Stadler, a true battler, and oil magnate's son Hal Sutton, once tipped to be the next Jack Nicklaus, were to prove stubborn opposition in a gritty if somewhat undistinguished match.

Stadler's 12 ft birdie putt did the damage on the second green, but the Americans missed a glorious chance of going two up on the next. It took the Europeans three messy shots and one good chip to reach the green, but after the visitors three-putted, Clark sank a five footer for a half in bogeys.

It obviously heartened the Europeans because they squared the match on the par five fourth when Clark arrowed his first shot, and his team's second, to within 12 inches.

A bogey five was enough to claim the sixth because Stadler put his partner in one of the many lakes inside the course. It was back to all square again on the next when a par three was enough for the Americans after Torrance had bunkered Clark.

Hal Sutton and Craig Stadler

Everybody had expected a real scrap, but not such scrappy play. Clark and Torrance's fourth bogey on the eighth gave the Americans the lead again as the two pairs continued to throw holes at one another.

An enormous roar greeted Torrance's tee shot on the 10th which faded beautifully on to the green à la Ballesteros. Two putts later the match was again level – a situation which existed for only as long as it took to play the next hole. Torrance's approach left Clark with a 50 ft putt which he steered to within three, but still too far for Torrance.

Clark raised European hopes when he holed an enormous putt on the next, but although the match was again all square with only six holes left, the Americans needed just four of them to claim victory by three and two.

Jacklin, having had the start he wanted, had anything but the finish he longed for after the morning foursomes. The Americans led by three points to one. Some rapid re-thinking was necessary.

FRIDAY FOURBALLS

Way & Woosnam v Zoeller & Green

1. FRIDAY / FOURBALLS

PLAYERS	1	2	3	4	5	6	7	8	9	OUT	10	11	12	13	14	15	16	17	18	IN	TOTAL	
WAY	4		4		3	4	3			32	3	4		4	3				3	36		
WOOSNAM		3		4	3								3			4	4	4		32	64	WIN
	A|S	+1			+2		+1	+2		+3		+2	+1						+1/2			1 HOLE
ZOELLER	4	4	4	4		4	3	3		34		4		3	3	4	3		4	31	65	
GREEN						4				4			4		2			4			A|S	

Paul Way's partnership with Ballesteros had been one of the major successes of the '83 Ryder Cup in America. It proved an inspirational pairing by Jacklin. Way was 20 at the time – a tough, gutsy competitor... and he showed why many were tipping him to someday reach the top.

Way started the '85 season in superb form and secured his Ryder Cup place before a severe bout of tonsilitis affected his health and form. He entered the competition having failed to make the last day in six out of the previous seven European events. "When the team was announced I could hardly stand up I was so weak, but I wouldn't have played had I thought I would let anybody down," he said.

Way completed a strenuous programme of fitness work and with the help of his new partner – the Welsh wonder Ian Woosnam – he was in reasonable shape when the announcer commanded him to the tee.

Any doubts about his health were quickly dispelled and Way's partnership with Woosnam – another tenacious fighter – was to bring instant dividends in this, their debut together.

They dovetailed superbly. Way produced the solid pars while Woosnam hit the Americans with birdies on the second, fourth and sixth holes. Zoeller, very much the senior partner alongside Green, also birdied the fourth and when the teams stood on the eighth tee, Europe were two up.

Zoeller's nine ft birdie putt trimmed the lead to one, but Way sank a 20-footer on the ninth to restore the advantage and then rammed home from nine feet on the 10th to create a three-hole lead.

Green's first birdie on the 12th – his tee shot finishing four ft from the pin – and Zoeller's 10 ft birdie putt on the next started to shade a different complexion on the match.

Zoeller's putter was now leaving scorch marks on the green and when he holed from 15 ft on the 16th the match was back to all square. Both sides birdied the 17th – Woosnam with two putts from cricket pitch length and Green with one from 15 ft. It all rested on the last.

When Way stood over a tricky downhill putt of 11 ft it seemed the match must finish all square, but the ball never looked like missing. It was a crucial point for the Europeans and prompted Woosnam to say: "If I could putt like Paul we'd beat anybody in the world together."

After the disappointment of going into lunch three-one down, Europe could not have had a better start to the afternoon.

Ballesteros & Pinero v North & Jacobsen

2 FRIDAY / FOURBALLS

PLAYERS	1	2	3	4	5	6	7	8	9	OUT	10	11	12	13	14	15	16	17	18	IN	TOTAL
	4	4	4	5	4	4	3	4	4	36	4	4	3	4	3	5	4	4	36		
BALLESTEROS	4	4		4	3	3	3			35	3		3	4	3	5		4			
			5					5	4			3					4				WIN
PINERO					A|S	+1					+1	+2		+1				+2			2+1
NORTH	3		5	4	4	3	4	4		35	4	4		4		5		5			
		4											3	2	4						
JACOBSEN	+1							A|S													

The Spanish connection – Ballesteros and Pinero

When the tall, rangey North bent over a five ft putt on the first hole it would have been difficult to push a wine bottle between the ground and the bottom of his hands, so low was he holding the putter. His unorthodox stance, some would say ugly with his feet a yard apart, was nevertheless effective. The ball dropped and Europe were one down.

The 579 yd fourth hole found Ballesteros bunkered with his three-wood approach and when North wedged to six inches, it was obvious something special was needed from the handsome Spaniard. Sevvy did not disappoint, coming out of the trap to only two inches for a birdie four and a half.

A typically huge drive and a nine iron second left Ballesteros just two-and-a-half feet from the hole at the next. The Americans could not answer his birdie and Europe were level.

Ballesteros's third successive birdie put Europe one ahead after six, but when he drove into water and Pinero found a bunker on the eighth, an unspectacular par was enough for North to square the match.

The gallery erupted behind the 275 yd par four 10th when Ballesteros pulled out a three wood and drilled his ball 23 ft from the pin. Two putts later Europe were one up for the first time – a lead they did not surrender.

Pinero's four foot birdie putt on the 11th doubled Europe's advantage to two holes and Ballesteros got up and down from a bunker at the next to protect it.

The Europeans were not amused when Jacobsen, a most personable man and popular player, pitched in from 35 yds for a birdie two which reduced the American deficit to one hole.

As they stood on the 17th tee the position was the same, but Ballesteros showed proof that he plays with his head as well as from instinct. His drive at the 575 yd par five was not good enough to give him the chance of reaching in two, so he laid up short of the danger with a five iron and then wedged to eight ft. One putt brought a winning birdie, his fifth, and the overall match situation was again level. The Spanish Armada was at full sail for Europe, although Ballesteros admitted he was feeling the strain.

"I like matchplay," he said. "It suits my game. But golf is difficult enough when you are playing for yourself . . . when you are also playing for Europe it is so much more difficult."

Langer & Canizares v Stadler & Sutton

3 FRIDAY / FOURBALLS

PLAYERS	1	2	3	4	5	6	7	8	9	OUT	10	11	12	13	14	15	16	17	18	IN	TOTAL
LANGER	4				4		4	4		36	3	3	3	4	3	4			4	32	68
CANIZARES	A\S	4	4	5	4		3			A\S +1							4	4		HALVED	
STADLER	4	4		4		4		4		35			3	3			4	4		33	68
SUTTON			4	+1	4		3	4			4	4		A\S	3	4	4				

Langer had lost his partner from the morning foursomes, the out-of-form Faldo, and now found himself alongside the third of the Spanish quartet, Jose-Maria Canizares.

A quiet, undemonstrative man known more for his consistency than flair, Canizares was to prove an able partner for the brilliant Langer, second only to Ballesteros in terms of world supremacy.

Altogether, it was not a spectacular match, although Langer proved conclusively that he can be just as breathtakingly brilliant as Ballesteros.

Langer halved the first with Stadler in regulation figures, but it was Canizares who assumed the role of principal partner over the next four. He produced solid pars each time, losing the fourth hole to Stadler's birdie when he wedged to three feet.

The Europeans were still one down at the turn but Langer stepped up to demonstrate his undoubted class. Approach shots to both the 10th and 11th greens finished four feet from the pin.

Single putts brought successive birdies, two wins... and a one hole lead.

Langer's third successive three was not enough to take the 12th but when Stadler struck from 15 ft at the next, the match was again all square... and destined to remain that way.

Sutton and Langer both birdied the 15th, Canizares and Stadler the 17th, both with chips and single putts. When Langer and Stadler parred the last, the two sides shook hands on a half. It was still neck and neck in the Ryder Cup.

Langer congratulates Canizares

Torrance & Clark v Floyd & Wadkins

4. FRIDAY / FOURBALLS.

PLAYERS	1	2	3	4	5	6	7	8	9	OUT	10	11	12	13	14	15	16	17	18	IN	TOTAL
TORRANCE			5	4				4	3	33	3		3			4		5		34	67
♦ CLARK	3	4	5		3	2							4		4	3		4	4		
	+1							A|S													
FLOYD	4		4		4		4	4	33		4	3	4		4		5	4		33	66
♦ WADKINS.		3	4		4	2						3			3	3				WIN 1 HOLE	
		A|S	+1	+2		+1										+1					

In Torrance, a proud Scot, and Clark, an equally proud Yorkshireman, Europe had a courageous partnership that was highly talented with it. In Floyd and Wadkins, two dour scrappers, America had the toughest of pairings. The match had the makings of a long, hard struggle. Nobody was surprised when it was.

Clark struck an early blow, holing from 10 ft for a first hole birdie. Wadkins countered on the second by stroking a six-footer

87

into the centre of the hole. And so it continued. Thrust and counterthrust. The faces of the Europeans mirrored their delights and disappointments. The faces of the Americans, whether in triumph or failure, resembled those of Mafia hit men who had just been handed a contract.

After four the Americans were two up – a par good enough to take the third, when both Clark and Torrance went on expeditions into jungle and desert, while Floyd claimed the fourth with a single putt birdie.

Clark calmly rolled in a birdie on the sixth to win the hole and followed it with another on the next. But so did Wadkins.

Torrance's putter did not catch fire until the ninth when a superb 20-footer squared the match. And there were more ear-blasting cheers when he unleashed every ounce of power he could summon to drive the 10th. But Wadkins, who had taken a safer route to the protected green, holed a 20-footer for a half in birdies.

The deadlock remained until the 16th when Wadkins snaked in a putt of almost 10 yards for a birdie which was to prove conclusive.

The next two holes were halved and the Americans claimed the match, a titanic tussle, by just one hole. They were ahead again, but the Europeans had them in view.

Torrance is congratulated by Jacklin

SATURDAY FOURBALLS

Torrance & Clark v Kite & North

1 SATURDAY FOURBALLS

PLAYERS	1	2	3	4	5	6	7	8	9	OUT	10	11	12	13	14	15	16	17	18	IN	TOTAL
	4	4	4	3	4	4	3	4	4	36	4	4	3	4	3	5	4	5	4	36	72
TORRANCE	4			5		4	3		4	35		4	3	4	3	5		4		36	72
& CLARK		3	4		3			5			3					4	3				WIN
	A|S	+1		+2				+1			+2		+1			+1	+2				2+1
KITE	4	5	5	4	4		4		36	4	4	2			5	4	4				
& NORTH		3				3		4					3	3							
														A|S							

The European pair had lost both their matches on the first day, but Jacklin kept faith. They were to repay him handsomely, in a match short of neither interest nor golf theatre.

Clark's nerves were tested on the second and he was found to have a steady hand. North chipped in from 30 ft leaving the blond, powerfully built Yorkshireman to assess a six ft putt for a half in birdies. Clark's judgement was perfect and he was to be rewarded on the next. Kite failed to equal his par when he needed to get down from 10 ft after being bunkered by his approach.

It was Clark again on the fifth who proved that no matter how many times he twitches and tugs his trousers before he putts, when the stroke is delivered it is as fluent as a metronome. His 20-footer put Europe two up.

It wasn't his sleeves that Torrance rolled up at the eighth, but his trousers. His second shot finished in water, but he managed to splash out only to take three putts while Clark had bunker and chipping problems. The hole was gifted to the Americans and the deficit reduced to one hole. Clark's 15 ft birdie putt on the 10th restored the two hole advantage. Kite, playing unspectacularly but still better than North, pulled one back on the 12th with his first birdie of the match.

North's second major contribution to the game was a three ft birdie putt on the 13th which levelled the contest, but Clark had not finished his birdie barrage. His fourth came on the 15th thanks to a monster 55-footer and when he chipped in from 20 ft on the next Europe were dormy two. Although Kite birdied the 17th, so did Torrance and the match was over. The chinks in the American armour were widening.

Way & Woosnam v Green & Zoeller

2 SATURDAY FOURBALLS

PLAYERS	1	2	3	4	5	6	7	8	9	OUT	10	11	12	13	14	15	16	17	18	IN	TOTAL
	4	4	4	5	4	4	3	4	4	36	4	4	3	4	3	5	4		4	36	72
WAY		4	4			4	3		5	34					3	5					NIN
r	3			4	3			4			4	4	2	4							43
WOOSNAM	+1		+2	+3	+4			+5	+4			+3	+4								
GREEN	4			5			3			38	4	3		4	3	5					
r		4	5		4	4		5	4				3								
ZOELLER																					

It was very much a case of "The Way we were" when the Europeans set out to prove their success of the previous afternoon had been no fluke. But this time it was Woosnam wielding the magic putter.

A 30-footer on the first straightened the ever-smiling Zoeller's face and before long the Americans were to discover the origins of Hurricane Gloria.

Woosnam and Way

Although a straight forward par was enough at the third to produce a two hole lead, Woosnam bagged birdies at the next two. The Americans were four down after only five holes . . . and wondering what had hit them.

Zoeller's drive on the eighth threatened the ducks more than the fairway and with Green bunkered, Woosnam's par was enough to establish a five hole lead.

It was the Europeans' turn to find sand and water on the ninth and Zoeller accepted the crumb of comfort. Green pulled it back to three down with a 24 ft putt for a birdie at the 11th. Woosnam replied with a tee shot which threatened the hole on the short 12th and his three ft putt signalled the re-establishment of a four hole lead.

All the Europeans needed to do was keep their heads. They did. The Americans could not better three successive pars and the pairs shook hands on the 15th green. Europe were ahead again. Surprisingly it was not to be for long.

Ballesteros & Pinero v O'Meara & Wadkins

3 SATURDAY FOURBALLS

PLAYERS	1	2	3	4	5	6	7	8	9	OUT	10	11	12	13	14	15	16	17	18	IN	TOTAL
BALLESTEROS	4	4	4	5	4	4	3	4	4	36	4	4	3	4	3	5	4	5	4	36	72
			4	5	4	4	3	4		36	3		3			4					
PINERO	4	4							4			4		4	2	4					
O'MEARA			4		4	3		4		32	4	3				5					WIN
WADKINS	3	4		5		2		3			3			3	3	4					3+2
	+1				+2	+3		+4						+5	+4	+3					

"Wadkins is the toughest of the Americans," said Jacklin. This match was to prove his feelings correct . . . and for the first time in the tournament put a cross on the Spaniards' examination paper.

The Europeans were for once powerless against the remorselessness of Wadkins and the coolness of O'Meara. When Wadkins calmly rolled in a 30-footer on the first it was to establish a lead the Americans never surrendered. The pairs exchanged pars for the next four holes and then the Americans bombed Europe with three birdies in four holes.

O'Meara sank one from seven ft at the sixth, Wadkins from 10 ft at the seventh and then again from twice that range at the ninth.

Ballesteros and Pinero were four down at the turn without dropping a stroke to par. Even when Ballesteros drove the 10th again a birdie was still not good enough to claim the hole – Wadkins putting his approach to six ft and holing out.

Wadkins holed again from eight ft at the 13th to leave Ballesteros and Pinero with nothing left to fight for but their pride. Five down with only the same to play. Pinero delayed the inevitable by holing from 45 ft on the 14th while Ballesteros won the next with a birdie. It was all over on the 16th, but at least the margin, three and two, was not as damaging to European morale as it might have been.

Langer & Lyle v Stadler & Strange

4 SATURDAY FOURBALLS.

PLAYERS	1	2	3	4	5	6	7	8	9	OUT	10	11	12	13	14	15	16	17	18	IN	TOTAL
	4	4	4	3	4	4	3	4	4	36	4	4	3	4	3	5	4	5	4	36	72
LANGER	3	4						5		34	3										
&				4	5	3	4		3			4	3	4	3	5	4	3	4		
LYLE	+1			A/S				A/S										A/S		HALVE	
STADLER			4	4			2	4		34				3			4	5			
&	4	3			4	4		5				3	4	2		4	5	3			
STRANGE		A/S		+1			+1						+1	+2	+1		+2	+1			

The last match of the Saturday morning foursomes was the one which Jacklin was to say: "Gave Europe the biggest boost we could ever have wished for."

Jacklin had been forced to play musical chairs with Langer because of the indifferent form of Faldo and his desire to partner Jose-Maria Canizares and Rivero later. When the music stopped this time, Lyle was alongside the West German.

Lyle had been "disappointed and angry" at being dropped from the Friday fourballs, but his greatest annoyance was at his own form. Fortunately he had sorted out the problem on the practice ground and approached the tee in a better frame of mind.

But it was Langer who struck the first blow. The Americans didn't even ask him to take out his putter when his approach shot to the first green finished just 18 inches from the pin. It was a significant distance because the entire match would eventually be decided by a putt of such length.

When Lyle missed from five ft at the second, Strange accepted the chance to square the match when he holed from two ft. The Americans were ahead after four when Stadler conjured a birdie from the par five with an eight ft putt, but Lyle immediately answered it with a birdie on the next.

The cat and mouse game continued with Stadler holing from 15 ft for a two at the seventh while a thunderous roar greeted Lyle's 13 ft birdie putt at the ninth to square the match.

Both Langer and Strange birdied the 10th, but the Europeans were unequal to the task as Strange rapped home a nine ft putt on the 12th and Stadler followed it with another winning birdie from similar distance on the next.

A par three won Lyle the 14th when Strange pulled his tee shot left and Stadler three-putted from the fringe, but the two-hole difference was restored on the 16th. Strange's six iron approach finished a foot from the flag. So with two holes left, the Europeans had to win both for a half in the match.

It looked all over when Stadler birdied the 17th. But two mighty blows had left Lyle standing over a 22ft eagle which, to Langer's delight and Europe's ecstasy, he holed.

And so to the last. Both Langer and Lyle missed birdie putts and looked to have lost all hope when Stadler lagged his 55 ft first effort to just 18 in. In normal circumstances the putt would have been conceded, but the match rested on it. Stadler was asked to putt out and unbelievably stabbed the ball wide.

A remarkable half point for Europe, but one which was worth incalculably more. It was at that moment that many shrewd observers of the game believed America had lost the Ryder Cup.

Stadler misses the vital putt

Sandy Lyle's Ryder Cup epitomised the performance of the European team. He started badly, improved in the middle and finished gloriously.

As the newly-crowned Open champion the amiable Shropshire lad was viewed with a new respect before the Belfry contest began. He was one of Europe's trump cards and felt the weight of responsibility. "I think people were looking to me to get at least three points," he recalls.

The first morning's play brought such patriotic optimists down to earth. It was, in the words of captain Tony Jacklin, "The Rude Awakening."

Lyle was paired with Ken Brown against Lanny Wadkins and Raymond Floyd in the first of the opening foursomes. Of the three European losses before lunch their four and three defeat was the most disheartening.

"Neither of us played very well and we just couldn't get going," said Lyle, "It was my responsibility to hit the long irons, particularly at the par three holes and I didn't do it as well as I can. The Belfry is the type of course which makes you look stupid if you're not playing well – and that's what it did to us."

The scoring reflected their troubles. Even though the Americans laboured to the turn in two over par 38 they still found themselves three up. Lyle and Brown, out in a disastrous 41, were six over par when the match finished at the 15th.

Jacklin immediately dropped them both for the afternoon fourballs, presenting the tabloids with their big story of the day.

"Sandy Row," screamed one back page in which Lyle was quoted: "If I'm not playing in tomorrow's fourballs I'll really have something to scream about. I'm sick at being dropped."

Such an untypical outburst from the normally mild-mannered Midlander demanded an explanation. "I was disappointed and annoyed," said Lyle, "But there was no argument with Tony. He came to me and said 'I'm leaving you out this afternoon' and I said 'That's fair enough'.

"I was upset because I'd played so badly. I felt I'd let myself down. It was the first day and as Open champion I knew that so much was expected of me. Having the afternoon off gave me the chance to sort myself out and get my mental attitude right."

For nearly two hours Lyle worked on his swing. He discovered he had been placing the ball two inches too far forward, causing a tendency to pull or cut. By Saturday morning he was striking the ball better. And it showed.

Lyle's partnership with US Masters champion Bernhard Langer secured a half against Craig Stadler and Curtis Strange to square the overall contest at six-six.

The match will forever be remembered for Stadler's missed putt on the 18th green. Yet the build-up to that dramatic moment – and Lyle's part in it – were important, too.

Some high-quality play, with both teams out in 34, had left them all square at the turn. Then Strange struck a telling blow at the 16th. His approach stopped a foot from the pin to set up a birdie three, which left the Americans dormy two up with two to play.

Anticipating that he needed an eagle three at the 575-yard par five 17th, Lyle went for a big drive across the corner of the dog-leg. He struck the shot perfectly only to see it hit a spectator's umbrella and drop in the light rough 40 yards short of its probable finishing point.

Instead of attacking the pin from the centre of the fairway Lyle was forced to play for the centre of the green, fading the ball back slightly towards the flag but still leaving himself a 12-yard putt.

"I knew I had to hole that one," Lyle recalled. Confirming his reputation as an excellent long putter, the Open champion duly rolled the ball in. The fourball was still alive.

Minutes later it died for the Americans. And so, almost certainly, did their hopes of retaining the Cup. After Lyle, with a 10 yarder, and Langer, with a 20-footer, had both missed birdie putts on the 18th to draw the match, Stadler rolled his to within two feet of the hole.

It was a gimme . . . almost. "I had a look at it," said Lyle, "And had we been out on the course, five down with five to play, I'd have conceded. But it was for victory on the final green so we had to make him play it."

Lyle was omitted again for the afternoon foursomes, a decision which, this time, did not disappoint him. "We were a 12-man team and it was right to give some of the others a chance," he said.

But he was back in the action on Sunday, playing his best golf of the week. Although his opponent Peter Jacobsen putted well to stay in touch, Lyle, out in two-under-par 34, was one up at the turn - and finished off his three and two victory in fine style.

For Lyle the euphoria capped a marvellous year. "Compared to winning The Open, the Ryder Cup competition was much harder," he said, "There was always that fear of letting the side down. We got there in the end because we put in a lot of concentration, had a marvellous team spirit and a great captain."

The Ryder Cup

The Trophy:
Samuel Ryder, twice Mayor of St Albans in Hertfordshire donated £100 to send a team of British pros to contest a match with their American counterparts in 1927. *Golf Illustrated* contributed £100 and the Royal & Ancient Golf Club of St Andrews sent £50.

The Contest:
Matchplay, comprising foursomes, fourballs and singles. Foursomes consists of teams of two playing strictly alternate shots. In fourballs both members of the two-man teams play each hole in its entirety.

The Teams:
Great Britain and Europe: Severiano Ballesteros *(Spain)*, Ken Brown *(Scotland)*, Jose-Maria Canizares *(Spain)*, Howard Clark *(England)*, Nick Faldo *(England)*, Bernhard Langer *(West Germany)*, Sandy Lyle *(Scotland)*, Manuel Pinero *(Spain)*, Sam Torrance *(Scotland)*, Jose Rivero *(Spain)*, Paul Way *(England)*, Ian Woosnam *(Wales)*. Non-playing captain: Tony Jacklin *(England)*.

United States of America: Ray Floyd, Hubert Green, Peter Jacobsen, Tom Kite, Andy North, Mark O'Meara, Calvin Peete, Craig Stadler, Curtis Strange, Hal Sutton, Lanny Wadkins, Fuzzy Zoeller. Non-playing captain: Lee Trevino.

How they were chosen:
Great Britain and Europe: Nine members of the team achieved automatic selection as a result of their performances and points gained from 18 tournaments starting with the Tunisian Open in April and ending with the Benson and Hedges International in mid-August. The captain, Tony Jacklin, personally selected the remaining three players: Ken Brown, Nick Faldo and Jose Rivero.
The United States: All 12 were selected on the points accumulated throughout the year to the USPGA Championship in early August. Points were awarded to the first ten places, with a greater number of points coming from the PGA Championship, the US Open and the Tournament Players' Championship. Winners of the PGA and US Open gains automatic selection, i.e. Andy North and Hubert Green.

The Score:
Great Britain and Europe 16½, U.S.A. 11½.

What it was all about

The Great Britain and European team: BACK (from left): Sam Torrance, Sevvy Ballesteros, Ken Brown, Nick Faldo, Sandy Lyle, Howard Clark, Jose-Maria Canizares, Manuel Pinero. FRONT (from left): Paul Way, Ian Woosnam, Tony Jacklin (non-playing captain), Bernhard Langer, Jose Rivero.

The USA team: BACK (from left): Lanny Wadkins, Fuzzy Zoeller, Calvin Peete, Mark O'Meara, Ray Floyd, Hal Sutton, Tom Kite, Curtis Strange. FRONT (from left): Hubert Green, Craig Stadler, Lee Trevino (non-playing captain), Andy North, Peter Jacobsen.

DAY ONE

FAR LEFT: Ballesteros goes for the flag

MIDDLE LEFT: Canizares blasts clear

BOTTOM LEFT: Ballesteros congratulated by Strange and O'Meara

LEFT: Way gets underway

RIGHT: Zoeller in a little trouble

CENTRE: Sutton lines it up with some weighty advice from Stadler

BOTTOM: Peete (left) and Kite (right) work out the distance

DAY TWO
FAR LEFT: Langer
crouches as Brown
considers

LEFT: Lyle's putter does
its job

BOTTOM LEFT:
A birdie for
Bernhard at the 15th

ABOVE: Joy for Clark
and Torrance (right),
also at the 15th

RIGHT: The
moment it all went
wrong for the USA –
Stadler misses from 18
inches on the 18th

North lines up a crucial putt

DAY THREE

LEFT: Woosnam talks it down

BOTTOM LEFT: Green leaves the tee

BOTTOM RIGHT: Pinero drives from the first

RIGHT: Jacklin (right)
hugs Pinero after the
shock defeat of
Wadkins

CENTRE: The faces of
defeat – O'Meara and
Trevino (right)

BOTTOM: One that got
away for Floyd

RIGHT: Torrance strides
onto the 18th to deliver
the coup de grâce

RIGHT: Yes! Torrance clinches it . . .

BOTTOM: . . . and celebrates in style

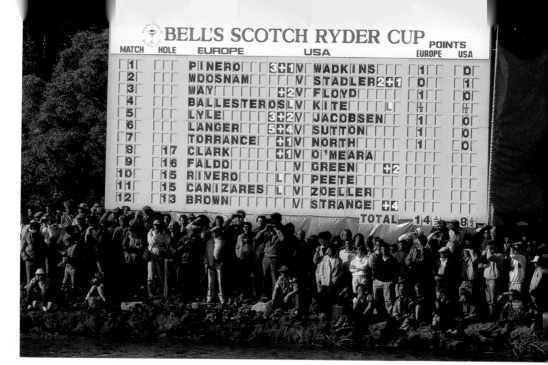

MATCH	HOLE	EUROPE		USA		POINTS EUROPE	USA
1		PINERO	3&1 V	WADKINS		1	0
2		WOOSNAM	V	STADLER	2&1	0	1
3		WAY	&2 V	FLOYD		1	0
4		BALLESTEROS	L V	KITE	L	½	½
5		LYLE	3&2 V	JACOBSEN		1	0
6		LANGER	5&4 V	SUTTON		1	0
7		TORRANCE	&1 V	NORTH		1	0
8	17	CLARK	&1 V	O'MEARA			
9	16	FALDO	V	GREEN	&2		
10	15	RIVERO	L V	PEETE			
11	15	CANIZARES	L V	ZOELLER			
12	13	BROWN	V	STRANGE	&4		
				TOTAL		**14½**	**8½**

ABOVE: The crucial scoreboard on Day 3

LEFT:
Jacklin tells the world how it was done

BOTTOM LEFT:
Trevino (left) summons a smile for Sevvy

LEFT: Torrance on
top of the world.

RIGHT: GB and Europe
show off the Cup

BOTTOM: Muchas
gracias – the Spanish
connection (from right)
Pinero, Ballesteros,
Canizares and Rivero

Sam Ryder's daughter at the victory presentation

RIGHT: Looking ahead to the next one (from left): Woosnam, Clark, Ballesteros, Torrance plus Jacklin, Way and Langer

Hail the chief:
Jacklin takes a bow, courtesy of Torrance

At The Belfry, September 13th, 14th and 15th, 1985.

FIRST DAY FOURSOMES

GREAT BRITAIN AND EUROPE	*Matches*	U.S.A.	*Matches*
S. Ballesteros and M. Pinero (2 and 1)	1	C. Strange and M. O'Meara	0
B. Langer and N. Faldo	0	C. Peete and T. Kite (3 and 2)	1
S. Lyle and K. Brown	0	L. Wadkins and R. Floyd (4 and 3)	1
H. Clark and S. Torrance	0	C. Stadler and H. Sutton (3 and 2)	1
	1		3

FOURBALLS

P. Way and I. Woosnam (1 hole)	1	F. Zoeller and H. Green	0
S. Ballesteros and M. Pinero (2 and 1)	1	A. North and P. Jacobsen	0
B. Langer and J. Canizares (halved)	0	C. Stadler and H. Sutton	0
S. Torrance and H. Clark	0	R. Floyd and L. Wadkins (1 hole)	1
	2		1

SECOND DAY FOURBALLS

S. Torrance and H. Clark (2 and 1)	1	T. Kite and A. North	0
P. Way and I. Woosnam (4 and 3)	1	H. Green and F. Zoeller	0
S. Ballesteros and M. Pinero	0	M. O'Meara and L. Wadkins (3 and 2)	1
B. Langer and S. Lyle (halved)	0	C. Stadler and C. Strange	0
	2		1

FOURSOMES

J. Canizares and M. Rivero (7 and 5)	1	T. Kite and C. Peete	0
S. Ballesteros and M. Pinero (5 and 4)	1	C. Stadler and H. Sutton	0
P. Way and I. Woosnam	0	C. Strange and P. Jacobsen (4 and 2)	1
B. Langer and K. Brown (3 and 2)	1	R. Floyd and L. Wadkins	0
	3		1

THIRD DAY SINGLES

M. Pinero (3 and 1)	1	L. Wadkins	0
I. Woosnam	0	C. Stadler (2 and 1)	1
P. Way (2 up)	1	R. Floyd	0
S. Ballesteros (halved)	0	T. Kite	0
S. Lyle (3 and 2)	1	P. Jacobsen	0
B. Langer (5 and 4)	1	H. Sutton	0
S. Torrance (1 hole)	1	A. North	0
H. Clark (1 hole)	1	M. O'Meara	0
N. Faldo	0	H. Green (3 and 1)	1
M. Rivero	0	C. Peete (1 hole)	1
J. Canizares (2 holes)	1	F. Zoeller	0
K. Brown	0	C. Strange (4 and 2)	1
	7		4

Match Aggregate: Great Britain and Europe, 15; U.S.A., 10 (3 halved).
Non-playing captains: T. Jacklin, Great Britain and Europe L. Trevino, U.S.A.

SATURDAY FOURSOMES

Canizares & Rivero v Kite & Peete

1 SATURDAY FOURSOMES

PLAYERS	1	2	3	4	5	6	7	8	9	OUT	10	11	12	13	14	15	16	17	18	IN	TOTAL
CANIZARES	4	4	4	5	4	4	3	4	4	36	4	4	3	4	3	5	4	5	4	36	72
	A|S	+1	A|S	H	+2		+3	+4			+5		+6	+7							
&	4	4	5	4	3	4	2	3	4	33	4	4	3	4							WIN
RIVERO																					7+5
KITE	4	5	4	5	4	4	3	7	4	40	5	4	4	5							
r																					
PEETE																					

Jacklin's decision to drop Torrance and Clark from the Saturday afternoon session raised more than a few eyebrows. They had beaten Kite and North in the morning and had developed into a formidable partnership.

But Jacklin's reasoning was both simple and unquestionable. He had to play Rivero before the Sunday singles – to have delayed his Ryder Cup debut until then would not only have been unfair but also unwise. And partnered by Canizares, Rivero had in fact won the World Cup for Spain.

Those who questioned the wisdom of the move only had to look at the scorecard for their answer. It showed a crushing seven and five triumph for the Europeans against a partnership which had outclassed Langer and Faldo in the Friday foursomes.

The early play gave little indication of the spectacular golf both Canizares and Rivero were to consistently hurl at their unsuspecting opponents. The Americans dropped a shot on the second and the Europeans on the third, but from the fourth tee to the eighth green, Rivero and Canizares pulverised the Americans with four birdies – every one good enough to win holes.

They reached the turn having taken just 33 shots against the Americans' four-over 40. A four-hole lead became five on the 10th when the Americans, for the third time in the match, found their ball smiling up at them from the depths of a lake.

Peete must have thought that he would have been better equipped with a pair of trunks than his waterproofs for tell-tale ripples on water close to the 12th hole told the story of another lost ball . . . and hole.

And it was all over on the 13th for although the Americans avoided water, they did find their ball buried in sand.

Their humiliation was complete while Rivero could not have asked for a finer start to his Ryder Cup career.

Ballesteros & Pinero v Stadler & Sutton

2 Saturday Foursomes

PLAYERS	1	2	3	4	5	6	7	8	9	OUT	10	11	12	13	14	15	16	17	18	IN	TOTAL
BALLESTEROS	A|S	+1	+2	+3		+4	+5	+6	+5	36	+4			+5	3	5	4	5	4	36	72
r PINERO	4	3	4	4	4	4	2	4	5	34	5	4	3	4	2					5&4 WIN	
STADLER	4	4	5	5	4	5	4	5	4	40	2	4	3	5	2						
r SUTTON																					

The Spaniards had lost their 100 per cent record in the morning fourballs. It had not undermined their confidence. They set off against Stadler and Sutton determined to prove that their defeat had been only a temporary hiccup. It took them only four holes.

The Americans were remorselessly ground into submission by a mixture of technical excellence on their opponents' behalf and some indifferent golf of their own.

Pinero, who is fond of reminding people: "There is more than one golfer in Spain" also showed that Langer is not alone in consistently frightening the flag with his approach shots.

A birdie claimed the second for Europe and if the world had been shocked by Stadler's miss from 18 inches in the morning, they were similarly stunned when Sutton found a two-footer too much for him on the third. When Ballesteros chipped to seven ft at the next and Pinero calmly rolled in the birdie, the Americans were three down with only four played.

Sutton studies the line

They slowed the onslaught on the next with a half, but then their problems intensified with every shot. Stadler must have been thinking of that 18 incher every time he took out his putter because he still could not read the greens while the Spaniards were inspired. With eight holes gone the Americans were six down and praying for a swift end to their misery.

They didn't so much win the ninth, as have it gifted while Sutton's drive on to the 10th green was sufficient to reduce the deficit to four down.

When Stadler drove out of bounds on the 13th he must have been wondering what else could go wrong with his day and when Ballesteros coaxed a four iron to two feet at the next the match was over. The Spaniards were sizzling again while the Americans were a shattered force.

Way & Woosnam v Strange & Jacobsen

3 SATURDAY FOURSOMES

PLAYERS	1	2	3	4	5	6	7	8	9	OUT	10	11	12	13	14	15	16	17	18	IN	TOTAL
	4	4	4	5	4	4	3	4	4	36	4	4	3	4	3	5	4	5	4	36	72
WAY r WOOSNAM	A|S				+1																
	4	4	4	5	3	4	4	5	5	38	5	5	4	4	2	5	4				
STRANGE r JACOBSEN	4	4	4	5	4	3	4	5	3	36	4	4	4	4	2	5	3			WIN	
						A|S		+1				+2	+3				+4			4&	2

Strange and Jacobson

Europe's "W" formation had been invincible in their previous two matches with wins over Zoeller and Green. "You can't really enjoy it while you're out there because it's work, hard work" said Way. "We don't really talk to one another much, but just get on with the job."

It was with that matter-of-fact, determined approach that Way, flicking his hair out of his eyes with a now typical twitch of his head, and Woosnam, round, solid and business-like, walked away from the first tee in search of a hat trick.

Strange, like Langer for the Europeans, had not had the same partner twice, but this time Trevino had found a winning combination in what was to prove the only success for the Americans on Saturday afternoon.

Way's successful five ft birdie putt on the fifth was the first time either side had broken par for a hole but it was a short-lived lead and one that was never to be regained. Jacobsen, tall, handsome and the epitome of the all-American boy, squared the match on the next when he found the length and line perfectly from 15 feet.

It was a similar story on the ninth, but from much closer and the Americans started the back nine one ahead.

Solid pars were good enough for the Americans to make severe inroads into European morale on the 10th and 11th and after four halved holes, the match ended on the 16th when Strange's approach finished 18 in from the hole.

Langer & Brown v Floyd & Wadkins

4 SATURDAY FOURSOMES

PLAYERS	1	2	3	4	5	6	7	8	9	OUT	10	11	12	13	14	15	16	17	18	IN	TOTAL
LANGER	4	4	4	5	4	4	3	4	4	36	4	4	3	4	3	5	4	5	4	36	72
+	A|S	+1	+2		+1		+1						+1			+2	+3			WIN	
BROWN	4	3	4	5	5	5	3	4	4	37	5	4	3	4	3	4	3				3+2
FLOYD	4	4	5	5	4	4	4	4	4	38	3	4	4	4	3	5	4				
+ WADKINS .					A|S				A|S												

Jacklin's respect for Langer and particularly the strength of his game, convinced him that, no matter the partner, Europe were always in with a chance in any game involving him.

But after three matches, Langer was still looking for his first win and one of his two halves had been gained thanks to Stadler missing a tiny putt.

Langer and Brown consider at length

Langer's fourth partner was Ken Brown, who hadn't played since the Friday morning and was not generally considered to be in top form. When it mattered, he found it.

It was a very close, tense affair against the poker-faced American pairing of Floyd and Wadkins. Neither Brown nor Langer are quick players. But they wouldn't be the players they are without attention to detail . . . and their meticulous approach was to pay handsomely.

Brown needed no reminding of the strength of the Americans for he had suffered against them, along with Lyle the day before. "It's very difficult to get your rhythm going when you are only playing alternate shots," said Lyle.

It was to prove similar this time, but fortunately for the Europeans, the Americans were even more afflicted by the long delays between shots.

Two up after three, thanks to Brown's immaculate wedge to the second green and Wadkins' missed 12 ft putt on the third, the Scot and West German were clawed back on the fifth and sixth when they parred neither. Both pairs were bunkered on the seventh, but while Langer and Brown got up and down in two, the Americans didn't.

It was all square again after 10, but when Wadkins missed from six ft on the 12th, the lead was surrendered again and never nullified. Langer's 18 ft putt on the 15th and Brown's eight iron approach shot to five inches on the next, produced a three and two win.

Jacklin had the two point lead he needed going into the last day.

SUNDAY SINGLES

Pinero v Wadkins

PLAYERS	1	2	3	4	5	6	7	8	9	OUT	10	11	12	13	14	15	16	17	18	IN	TOTAL
	4	4	4	5	4	4	3	4	4	36	4	4	3	4	4	5	4	5	4	36	72
	A|S			A|S				A|S				+1	+2			+3	+2	+3		WIN	N3+1
Pinero	4	4	5	5	4	5	3	4	4	38	3	3	3	4	3	4	4	5			
Wadkins	4	4	4	6	3	5	3	5	4	38	4	5	3	4	3	5	3	6			
			+1		+1																

The quiet, affable Spaniard had been squatting on the floor in one of the team rooms at The Belfry when Jacklin told him he would lead off the crucial singles. "When I told him he was playing Wadkins he jumped to his feet," said Jacklin. "He was delighted. Wadkins was the player he wanted."

Pinero had lost his 100 per cent record with Ballesteros, against Wadkins and O'Meara. This was the head to head he had dreamed about. And against the player Jacklin believed to be the toughest of the Americans in matchplay.

Even if the outcome had been different, Pinero would still have emerged from the tournament with a good record. Triumph here and he knew it would be excellent . . . and one which nobody could better, not even Ballesteros.

Few would have envied his task against Wadkins, but Pinero was to typify the spirit that ran through the length of the European side. He set off with only one thing in his mind – success. But he had twice to come from behind to achieve it.

Fortunately his lapse at the third when he needed three to get down from the fringe was not an indication of his overall play. The lost hole was immediately recovered when Wadkins drove into the front of a bunker on the par five fourth and needed another five shots to get down.

The disappointment turned to delight for Wadkins when he rammed home a 30 ft putt on the next to reclaim the lead. It was relinquished on the eighth when he couldn't get down in two from 25 ft. Pinero had his man where he wanted him and he hit him with every missile from his expansive armoury.

The shot that hurt most, although Wadkins' face was to tell as many tales as a stone slab, came on the 10th. Pinero was 35 ft from the pin and not on the green in two. Wadkins was staring at a possible birdie and comfortable par at worst. Pinero miraculously chipped in – proving that Ballesteros is not the only golfer capable of producing remarkable feats on this most picturesque of holes.

It must have hit Wadkins hard. He couldn't match the birdie, was behind for the first time in the match and the next hole showed he was clearly in a state of shock. While Pinero arrowed a two iron approach to 15 ft, Wadkins was first in a bunker and then a bush. Two down . . . and downhearted.

When Pinero wielded his magic putter again for a winning birdie on the 15th, Wadkins was three down and could escape only with a half at best. It needed a superhuman effort to avoid defeat. and he came up with the first leg when he birdied the 16th. But his hopes were buried in sand at the next and Pinero had sealed the victory that propelled Europe closer to history making.

With four points out of a possible five, Pinero was to become the leading points winner of the 12 heroes.

Manuel Pinero . . . out of the sand

Woosnam v Stadler

2.

PLAYERS	1	2	3	4	5	6	7	8	9	OUT	10	11	12	13	14	15	16	17	18	IN	TOTAL
	4	4	4	5	4	4	3	4	4	36	4	4	3	7	5	5	4	5	4	36	72
(status)	+1					A|S +1									A|S						
WOOSNAM	4	5	5	6	4	4	3	4	4	39	5	4	3	5	2	5	4	5			
STADLER	5	4	5	3	4	5	4	3	4	37	4	4	3	5	3	4	3	5			
(status)		A|S	+1			A|S			+1						H	+2				WIN	2+1

Jacklin had altered his final day stratagem after his experiences two years previously in Florida. Then, he had gone into the singles "With all guns blazing." Now he had decided to hold fire at the start and his pack top players into the centre of his team structure.

Pinero, although few would have considered him a banker bet against Wadkins, had given Jacklin the perfect start. Anything that "Woosie" could pick up against the stern Stadler would be an extra bonus.

The Americans, leading with their matchplay strong men while saving Strange and Zoeller as reliable anchor men, believed Stadler owed them one for his missed putt in the Saturday fourballs – an error which contributed to the team starting the final day two points behind instead of just one.

Stadler openly shows his displeasure when he isn't playing well or things are going against him. It would have taken a brave man to speak to him when he three-putted the first to go behind. Woosnam was similarly displeased when he did exactly the same on the second to lose his advantage.

Woosnam, as popular a player as there is on the European circuit, was kicking himself again on the fourth hole when he added another £1.50 worth to the £1,000's worth of golf balls submerged in Belfry waters. Stadler was the next to make ripples – on water and applause among the partisan crows – as he lost the sixth.

When he couldn't sink a putt of 15 ft on the seventh, Woosnam was ahead again, but only temporarily – Stadler finding life at last in his putter when a 10-yarder dropped on the eighth.

Woosnam was not at his best, but still giving Stadler a huge fight. He stood on the 13th tee one down and decided to play safe with an iron. He wished he'd taken wood when he pulled his tee shot out of bounds. Stadler only had a short pitch to the green, but casually plopped his ball into a greenside bunker. Having played three off that tee, Woosnam scrambled a birdie with his second ball and instead of being an expected two down was still only one.

It was just the spur Woosnam needed and when he holed a five footer from off the green for a winning two at the 14th, Stadler looked a beaten man.

The beauty of golf is that you can predict nothing. From being a devastated man, Stadler was suddenly inspired – winning the 15th and 16th with birdies and shaking hands on a two and one triumph after a par at the long 17th.

Stadler had had his revenge on the course while Woosnam had been beaten, but in no way disgraced. Indeed his performances and cheerful personality had ensured a rapid increase in his ever-growing fan club.

Way v Floyd

PLAYERS	1	2	3	4	5	6	7	8	9	OUT	10	11	12	13	14	15	16	17	18	IN	TOTAL
	4	4	4	5	4	4	3	4	4	36	4	4	3	4	3	5	4	5	4	36	72
WAY	+1				+2	+3	+2	+3	+4				+3	+2			+1				
WAY	4	4	5	4	4	5	3	4	4	37	4	5	4	4	3	5	5	5	W		2up
FLOYD	5	4	5	5	5	4	4	5	4	41	4	4	3	4	3	5	4	5	C		

You have only to look at Paul Way's forearms to see the amount of work he has put in to become a champion. They are like Popeye's – after the spinach. He had already performed with distinction alongside Woosnam despite his debilitating tonsilitis. Those who had wondered whether his recent poor form would make him the let-down of the European team had already been answered.

But now he was alone on the fairways with only his own thoughts and company. If he could have played against anybody who might have helped him relax, it certainly wasn't Floyd – an imposing, somewhat intimidating figure without the appearance of a natural athlete, but definitely with the game to test anybody's resolve.

Way must have thought his birthday and Christmas had arrived simultaneously as Floyd, winner in two of his previous three matches, moved from one disaster to another. Way had one birdie and two bogeys in an outward half of 37 – nothing particularly special. Yet Floyd was four down having staggered to the turn in an amazing 41 shots.

Floyd was staring down the barrel at humiliation. It says much for his pedigree that Way was taken to the 18th green before the trigger was pulled.

But if it spoke much of Floyd, it said more of Way. There can be fewer safer bets for major championship honours than this Middlesex-born 22-year-old, whose boyhood idol was Gary Player. "I practice Gary's power of positive thinking philosophy, too," says Way.

And he needed to call upon every last positive thought in his head during a back nine which saw Floyd mount a thrilling fight-back. The difference was still two holes with three to play. Floyd's drive at the 16th hooked into thick rough while Way was 15 yards further and, although off the fairway, sitting quite comfortably in the semi. Floyd took an age to play his shot and finally hacked it out 20 yards short of the green. Way, with what looked a simple pitch, incredibly almost split the ball in half—thinning it through the green into an almost unplayable position.

Floyd chipped dead for his par and won the hole. From looking in a position where he was almost certain to win the hole and the match, Way now found himself on the 17th tee only one up.

Ray Floyd with an uphill putt and an uphill task

More than one seasoned observer and some who should know better muttered: "He'll lose it now, you watch." We did and Way didn't. He settled his nerves with a half in par fives at the 17th and then watched Floyd put his tee shot into a bunker with his drive at the last.

Floyd had to go for a miracle and ended with a disaster – topping his bunker shot into the lake fronting the 18th green. With Way safely on in two, much to everybody's relief, Floyd had to concede the match.

Way had won an enormous battle with Floyd and himself. He had again proved what a superb Ryder Cup performer he is.

Ballesteros v Kite

PLAYERS	1	2	3	4	5	6	7	8	9	OUT	10	11	12	13	14	15	16	17	18	IN	TOTAL
	4	4	4	3	4	4	3	4	4	36	4	4	3	4	3	5	4	3	4	36	72
	A|S																	A|S		HALVED	
BALLESTEROS	4	4	5	6	4	4	3	4	4	38	4	3	3	5	2	4	4	4	4	33	71
KITE	4	3	5	5	4	4	4	4	3	36	4	3	3	4	3	5	4	5	4	35	71
		+1		+2			+1		+2					+3	+2	+1					

No wonder Jacklin said: "I wouldn't want to play Sevvy at matchplay for a living." This match offered everything – high drama, golf theatre at its best and concrete proof that there is no more dangerous animal in golf than Ballesteros when he is wounded.

Kite certainly hurt him and Ballesteros can rarely have had to dig as deep into his bag of tricks to conjure something special from very little.

The tough Texan was already well known among British Ryder Cup audiences. Sandy Lyle had fired eight birdies at him four years ago at Walton Heath and had left the course after 16 holes. Kite had answered Lyle's blitz with an incredible 10 of his own.

It should not have been too big a surprise then that with just five holes to play, Kite was three up. What was a shock was that he had achieved his position without producing anything much out of the ordinary for golf standards at this level. He had reached the turn in level par 36 against Ballesteros's 38. The two-hole lead became three on the 13th when the Spaniard, not for the first time, was seen anchoring his feet in a bunker.

Ballesteros had given no hint of what was to follow, but what did had his army of followers screaming with delight. He holed one of the longest putts of the tournament, from 45 ft, on the par three 14th and then sank another from 15 ft at the next to be just one down.

Now Kite was on the canvas, but he hauled himself far enough off it to stop the rot on the next when both players made par.

As the crowd held their breath on the 17th tee, Ballesteros held nothing back. His huge drive cut the corner and finished some 60 yards ahead of Kite and in the centre of the fairway. The American could not get up in two. Ballesteros could and his three wood approach never left the stick. Unfortunately it did depart the green through the back door and left a testing little chip.

It was the sort that Ballesteros normally leaves inches away or occasionally holes. This time it stopped 12 ft short. The cheers when that putt dropped must have been heard 10 miles away.

Within the space of four holes Ballesteros had hit three birdies to square the match. He put no pressure on Kite with his tee shot on the last, finishing in light rough with a formidable long iron shot left. Kite was some 50 yards closer to the hole having unleashed a brave and incredibly long drive.

The tension in the American camp showed as Stadler raced across the fairway to offer encouragement to his team-mate. Ballesteros, now deep in a tunnel of concentration, hit an excellent approach shot which just clawed its way to the correct level of the three tier green. Kite bettered it, leaving his ball 15 ft from the flag, but neither he nor Ballesteros could make the putts that would have brought outright victory.

A half it was, but what a morale booster for the Europeans.

Lyle v Jacobsen

PLAYERS	1	2	3	4	5	6	7	8	9	OUT	10	11	12	13	14	15	16	17	18	IN	TOTAL
	4	4	4	5	4	4	3	4	4	36	4	4	3	4	3	5	4	5	4	36	72
	A|S		+1					+1				+2	+1		+2	+3				WIN	
KYLE	3	4	4	5	4	4	2	4	4	34	4	4	3	5	3	4	3			3+2	
JACOBSEN	3	4	6	4	4	4	2	5	4	36	4	5	3	3	3	6	4				
			A|S																		

This was the pairing of two perfect gentlemen. Lyle acknowledged his opponent as: "Probably the nicest guy in the American team,"

Peter Jacobsen, that most gentlemanly of the American players, was one of several who spoke out against the blatant, if understandable, partisanship of some sections of The Belfry crowd. The U.S.A. team were particularly peeved by the huge roar of pleasure which greeted Craig Stadler's horrendous miss in the Saturday fourballs.

Said Jacobsen: "Losing the Ryder Cup did not bother me as much as the behaviour of the galleries. All that cheering when we missed shots. I've never known anything like it before, and especially not from a British crowd. You expect so much from them."

Jacobsen was also scathing about Lee Trevino's brand of captaincy. "Lee seemed to have nothing to say about anything at anytime," he said. "On the other hand the Europeans had Tony Jacklin rushing everywhere with a walkie-talkie and a miniature TV set. He knew exactly what was going on at any moment. Every time I looked he was on the course urging on his lads. If I were Europe I'd make him captain for the next 30 years. If they don't want him – give him to us. That man's a winner."

while many would say the same of the Open champion himself in the company of his European colleagues.

Neither had had the best of Ryder Cups, however. Lyle, as naturally gifted as any, lost his Friday foursomes and was gifted a half in the Saturday fourballs thanks to Stadler's miss from 18 inches. Jacobsen had done marginally better, winning one and losing one of his two previous matches.

But as Jacklin said afterwards: "Sandy came back and really climbed on the rails again," while the player himself in typical modest fashion, was to agree that he had finished on a nice note.

Both Lyle and Jacobsen, the latter having rugby tackled a streaker on the last green at The Open, hit an early hot streak themselves – each of them barging birdies at the first with 10 ft and eight ft putts respectively.

When Jacobsen not only found a bunker on the third, but also the rough on both sides of the fairway, Lyle went one up. He lost it on the next to a birdie, but regained the initiative again on the eighth when Jacobsen followed the path of many into water.

Lyle was playing very steadily indeed and had moved to two up before he committed his only error of the round – driving out of bounds on the 13th. It was not an unlucky omen for Jacobsen conceded the 15th after three-putting and then had to accept defeat as Lyle rolled in a 30-footer on the next for a three and two triumph.

Langer v Sutton

PLAYERS	1	2	3	4	5	6	7	8	9	OUT	10	11	12	13	14	15	16	17	18	IN	TOTAL
	4	4	4	5	4	4	3	4	4	36	4	4	3	4	3	5	4	5	4	36	72
	+1		+1	+2		+3	+2	+1	+2		+3	+4	+5	+4	+5						
LANGER	4	4	4	5	4	3	4	5	4	37	4	W	3	5	2					WINS	5&4
SUTTON	5	3	5	6	4	4	3	4	5	39	5	C	6	4	3						
		A|S																			

Jacklin's strategy of sandwiching his strength was paying off handsomely. What a player to have coming in to bat at six. Jacklin knew that Langer would not let him down.

He didn't. Pity then that Sutton, a most approachable young man with an excellent pedigree, should let himself down by belly-aching afterwards about the standard of behaviour among the Belfry galleries. Of course they wanted Europe to win, but they did it generally in good spirit and were never malicious.

One notable American journalist, when told of Sutton's outburst afterwards, said: "When he sees what he said in print tomorrow, he'll regret ever having said it. I'm afraid it's just a bag of sour grapes."

Perhaps Sutton was disappointed at his own form for Langer had produced nothing but par golf after four holes and was

Bernhard Langer

already two up. The fifth hole was remarkable for just one aspect – the two players' par fours producing the only halved hole of the entire match.

Langer followed a 45 ft birdie putt on the sixth with two bogeys which reduced his three hole advantage to just one, but he doubled it on the next when Sutton three putted from 18 ft.

Sutton was just not enjoying himself and Langer was five up after 12 without ever having to exert himself. Several Europeans had found trouble at the 13th, a 394 yd par four, and Langer was no exception. But the match was over on the next when Langer rifled a five iron to just 12 inches from the pin.

Torrance v North

PLAYERS	1	2	3	4	5	6	7	8	9	OUT	10	11	12	13	14	15	16	17	18	IN	TOTAL
	4	4	4	5	4	4	3	4	4	36	4	4	3	4	3	5	4	5	4	36	72
	A|S																	A|S			
TORRANCE	4	4	6	5	4	4	3	5	C	/	6	4	3	4	3	5	4	4	3		10up
NORTH	4	4	6	4	3	4	4	5	W	/	5	5	3	4	3	6	4	5	6		
				+1	+2		+1		+2		+3	+2			+1						

"Everybody feels pressure," said Sam Torrance's father Bob. "Winners are the ones who can cope with it." How Sam was to show the world what a winner he is. No wonder he was to leave the last green announcing: "This has been the greatest moment of my life."

Had a poll been taken asking golf followers to nominate the player they would most like to see win the point that claimed the Ryder Cup, Torrance's name would certainly have been high on the list.

A golfaholic and as tough a competitor as can be found outside Ballesteros and Langer in Europe, Torrance was paired alongside Andy North, a surprise double US Open winner. Neither was to know what awaited them on and around the 18th green, and after 10 holes, with North three up, whatever glory was to be had, it appeared that somebody other than Torrance would claim it.

"When I went three down I just told myself to keep concentrating, keep trying and hopefully my luck would change," said Torrance. It did on the next as North failed to find the green with his approach, chipped to eight feet and missed the putt.

But as the players stood on the 15th tee, North was still two up and European nerves were starting to twitch a little as the scoreboard showed American domination in most of the following matches.

North's chip to the green, his fourth shot, finished just two-and-a-half feet from the stick and looked good enough to secure another half. Incredibly, he missed and Torrance was reeling him ever closer.

Urged on by Jacklin, who informed Torrance what was required of him, the Scot attacked the 17th with what seemed like 20 years' accumulated adrenalin pumping through his veins. His second shot hooked into thick rough, but if every European heart sank, Torrance's certainly didn't. His recovery was one of the best witnessed throughout the three days. It finished just six feet from the pin when most wouldn't have given him a chance of ending six yards from the green.

Torrance needed to hole the putt for a win which would square the match. When it disappeared from sight, the roar was second only too the noise Concorde made when it joined the celebrations afterwards.

The determination was etched deep into Torrance's face, but surprisingly he was thinking anything but positive thoughts. "The first thing I thought of when I stood on the tee was my drive at the ninth which I'd topped 130 yards into the lake."

His mind was clear when he launched into the ball, however. It was the longest drive seen throughout the tournament, well over 300 yards and reducing the 474 yd monster par four to a measly nine-iron approach shot.

North had the disavantage of playing second knowing that Torrance was in perfect position. There were muted, but cruel cheers when he ballooned his drive. North knew where it was going to fall and the ripples on the lake confirmed his worst fears.

"As soon as it dropped in I knew we'd won the Ryder Cup," said Torrance. "I've never known such a feeling. I just burst into tears."

North refused to surrender, took a penalty drop, pitched short of the second lake and then arrived at the green in four shots. Torrance's face was getting wetter by the second, but he cleared his eyes long enough to swing his club and watch the ball float gently on to the green, resting about seven yards from the hole.

The American finished with a six. Torrance had three putts to write his name in the history books. He needed just one, immediately raising his arms to the crowd, unashamedly sobbing. He wasn't the only one. "I'll remember that putt as long as I live," he said. He need have no fears – nobody will let him forget it.

Yes Sam!

The Ryder Cup was won. The green was flooded by people led by Jacklin and the players who had finished. Torrance was not to know until later that somebody almost stole his thunder.

For Sam Torrance the honour of striking the winning shot brought instant pain and lasting pleasure. That night in the hotel swimming pool, buoyed up by a million champagne bubbles, Torrance attempted to float on air – and ended with such a heavy fall that he feared he had smashed his rib cage.

Severe bruising was diagnosed, and even a fortnight later he was still in agony each time he attempted a full blooded swing. But if the discomfort lingered, his delight just went on and on.

"Everywhere I go, I'm the man who won the Ryder Cup," he said ecstatically. "People stop me in the streets, call to me from cars. I've never known anything like it. Was the entire nation watching that putt?

"I've had my wonderful moments in golf. None can compare with that. My only regret is for Andy North. What a way for him to lose to me, driving into the lake. If I had known I was going to shoot that birdie on the 18th I would have given Andy a par as we stood on the tee. At least he would have gone down with plenty of pride.

"We've shown the public what we have known on the circuit for a couple of years . . . namely, European golf is the best in the world right now. We have Ballesteros, Langer, Lyle and a posse of other players capable of winning the greatest prizes. As for the Ryder Cup, we forged such a fantastic team spirit under Jacko that we must go to America in two years with real confidence of maintaining our premier position. By then perhaps this great feeling will have worn off."

Clark v O'Meara

PLAYERS	1	2	3	4	5	6	7	8	9	OUT	10	11	12	13	14	15	16	17	18	IN	TOTAL
	4	4	4	3	4	4	3	4	4	36	4	4	3	4	3	5	4	5	4	36	72
	+1			+2	+3			+2				+1									WIN
CLARK	4	4	5	4	4	4	3	4	C	/	4	4	4	4	3	5	4	5	4		1UP
O'MEARA	5	4	5	6	5	4	3	4	3	39	4	4	3	4	3	5	4	5	4	36	75

131

It will be interesting, in future years, to see how many golf follow-ers know which battles were being fought after Torrance had sea-led victory. Clark will definitely never forget, for he had the chance to upstage Torrance, his fourball and foursomes partner.

But even so Clark will always be able to look back with pride on the contribution he made to such a marvellous achievement. "Before, when I'd played in the Ryder Cup it had been in the com-pany of Watson and Nicklaus," he said. "You felt two down as soon as they walked into the same room. This time it was different. The Americans had nobody with that charisma."

So Clark must have approached the first tee at least feeling on level terms against O'Meara. And if he did, it was a position which was never to deteriorate.

After the first hole, Clark was never worse than one up. He was three up after five, but back to one after 12. And with both players making par at the last six holes, that is how it finished.

The only real drama of a very close struggle came on the 17th with Clark standing over a putt of about four feet. At this stage, Torrance was sizing up the putt that was eventually to prove the decider. But had Clark sunk his, the match would have been over before Torrance addressed his ball. Clark missed. The glory was Torrance's.

Howard Clark wins his singles on the 18th

Faldo v Green

9

PLAYERS	1	2	3	4	5	6	7	8	9	OUT	10	11	12	13	14	15	16	17	18	IN	TOTAL
	4	2	4	5	4	4	3	4	4	36	4	6	3	4	3	5	4	5	4	36	72
		A|S				+1															
FALDO	5	3	5	4	5	3	3	6	5	39	4	5	4	4	2	5	5	6			
GREEN	4	4	5	4	5	5	3	4	4	38	4	5	3	4	3	5	4	5		WIN	
	+1							A|S	+1				+2	+1			+2	+3		3	+1

Faldo's selection should have surprised nobody. His previous Ryder Cup record was good enough to earn him Jacklin's nod and invitation. But there were those who thought Faldo should have sat this competition out, that others had done more over the previous year to warrant selection.

Certainly, Faldo arrived at The Belfry without a win for the season and with a new swing. Few had seen much wrong with the old one. To see Faldo practising meticulously checking every detail, was to watch a golfer not at peace with himself.

His thousands of British followers were hoping that the Ryder Cup would help his confidence return . . . and with it the form he has shown so consistently before. It was not to be.

After failing, alongside Langer, in the foursomes of the first morning, this was the first time he has been called into action since. Would a semblance of consistency return against Green? The first six holes told their own story – bogey, birdie, bogey, birdie, bogey, birdie. The ecstacy and agony in triplicate.

When he dropped three shots on the last two holes of the outward half, Faldo was one down and never to recover. Green, having played little better, ran out a winner by three and one, having dropped three shots over the 17 holes played.

Rivero v Peete

10

PLAYERS	1	2	3	4	5	6	7	8	9	OUT	10	11	12	13	14	15	16	17	18	IN	TOTAL
	4	4	4	5	4	4	3	4	4	36	4	4	3	4	3	5	4	5	4	36	72
	A|S	1						+1	+2		+1		+1		+2	+1					
RIVERO	4	4	5	5	4	5	3	5	3	38	4	5	3	4	3	5	4	5	4	37	75
PEETE	4	4	5	5	4	5	3	6	4	40	3	4	4	4	4	3	4	4		34	74
												A|S					1	A|S	+1	WINS UP	

Rivero, like Faldo, was playing only for the second time, but in his case he was now defending a 100 per cent record – his seven and five victory with Canizares over Kite and Peete representing the biggest win of all the 28 matches.

Peete, a man of few words, but many shots, had the chance to regain his self respect while Rivero had the opportunity to convincingly answer those who doubted the wisdom of his selection.

It was not a match of inspired golf, but it was enthralling. The pair had matching figures for a surprising seven holes while a bogey was enough for Rivero to break the deadlock on the eighth. A birdie on the next sent him to the turn two up having played 38 shots to Peete's 40.

The match was level after 11, but Rivero was again two up after 14. It was cruel for the plucky Spaniard that Peete should birdie the next three holes to take the lead and hold on to it down the last.

Canizares v Zoeller

PLAYERS	1	2	3	4	5	6	7	8	9	OUT	10	11	12	13	14	15	16	17	18	IN	TOTAL
	4	4	4	5	4	4	3	4	4	36	4	4	3	4	3	5	4	5	4	36	72
	A|S			+1				A|S										+1	+2		
CANIZARES	3	4	5	4	4	4	3	C	4		4	4	3	4	3	5	4	5	3	WIN	2UP
ZOELLER	3	4	5	5	4	3	3	3	5	35	4	4	3	4	3	5	4	6	C		
						A|S		+1													

Pinero congratulates a delighted Canizares – another European victory

Canizares had only scraped into the team, but like the other Spaniards was to justify his place. Although lacking the flamboyance and charisma of Ballesteros, and at 38 the 'old man' of the side, he was nevertheless considered a dependable ally to the cause.

His consistency from tee to green has been one of the hallmarks of his game and in 1984 he had taken first place in the 'greens to regulation' category with an outstanding 79 per cent.

The pairing with Zoeller was that of opposites. The American is rarely to be seen without a smile on his face or a song on his lips, on or off the course. Canizares is a much more serious character, but he was to have the last laugh in a match which went to the final green.

Zoeller hit Canizares with four threes in the front nine, but still could not break clear. The pair turned for home all square and matched each others pars for the first seven inward holes.

The American made the first mistake . . . and it was to prove fatal. He bogeyed the 17th and Canizares was assured of at least a half. He made sure it was a full point on the last when he escaped trouble and Zoeller didn't.

With two-and-a-half points out of a possible three, Canizares could look back with much satisfaction on his contribution. Indeed he was the only European not to suffer defeat throughout the three days.

Brown v Strange

PLAYERS	1	2	3	4	5	6	7	8	9	OUT	10	11	12	13	14	15	16	17	18	IN	TOTAL
	4	4	4	5	4	4	3	4	4	36	4	4	3	4	3	5	4	5	4	36	72
	A|S																				
BROWN	4	4	5	5	6	5	3	4	3	39	5	4	3	3	3	4	4				
STRANGE	4	4	4	4	4	4	3	4	3	34	4	5	3	3	3	5	3				
			+1	+2	+3	+4					+5	+4				+3	+4		WIN	4	+2

The last match of the competition and one of five which was eventually to have no significance to the destiny of the trophy. With hindsight, Trevino might well have promoted Strange in his order. But there was no turning back once he had handed in his team-sheet and he had decided to start and end with his big guns.

The superb consistency of the American was to prove too much for Brown in a one-sided contest which nevertheless did not end until the 16th green.

Apart from being bunkered on the first and still making par, Strange played flawlessly in a front nine which included two birdies and no bogeys. After 10, he was five ahead and Brown was staring at possibly the biggest reverse of the three days. To his credit he refused to surrender, winning the 11th and matching Strange's three threes at the next three holes.

He stayed alive by winning the 15th, but couldn't beat Strange's birdie on the 16th. The battle was lost, but the war was over and it would be Brown, not Strange, celebrating victory.

7 *Ryder Cup Diary*
by Peter Dobereiner

September 10.

Summer has arrived at last. It is a gorgeous day at Pratts Bottom, for which I am thankful because it is Roger Fidler's benefit pro-am at my golf club, West Kent, and Roger has been a good friend for 25 years. The members have rallied around loyally and there should be a good turnout. Driving up to the club on the Old Dover Road, where highwaymen once lurked among the beech trees, I get a sharp attack of Golf Writer's Cringe. This is an occupational stress disorder caused by the standard response of strangers when they learn what you do for a living. "You go all over the world covering golf tournaments? What a wonderful life! Do you want somebody to carry your bag?" Well, the life does have its compensations but there is another side to the coin.

For the thousandth time I do a mental calculation. One wife, four children and 25 years on the road. That makes 150 family celebrations, birthdays and anniversaries. Well, not quite because all the kids were not born the day we were married but it must be over 100. I have been at home for eight of them. Now I am going to miss Roger's big day.

At least I have time to wish him well and raise a glass of champagne before getting back into the car and heading for the Dartford Tunnel. I do another calculation based on Murphy's Law and hard experience of motorway contractors' incompetence: the final section of the M25 will be opened on the day I retire. I cheer myself up by anticipating a notable double, victory in the Ryder Cup and a grandson on the same day. That would exorcise a national golfing curse and the family curse of an equally frustrating run of 28 years of nothing but girls.

At The Belfry I get out my gate entry card but nobody wants to see it. The gate entry card is a relatively recent example of bureaucratic pomposity which makes someone, somewhere, feel important. If they sent out a badge and a parking sticker at least you would know where to leave the car. I park in the usual spot and within seconds a lout on a fork-lift truck hits my car a glancing blow and breaks the orange glass on my flasher. What a wonderful life!

Most of the usual crowd are already hammering out their pre-previews, pausing briefly to exchange the ritual corny insults. Fleet Street is becoming more and more obsessed with telling readers what is going to happen. I go out to inspect the course before the anticipated hordes make walking impossible. The Americans are out getting their first feel of The Belfry, loudly exchanging their impressions with a forced bonhomie. They cannot fault the conditions; Brian Cash, the director of The Belfry, has done a wonderful job of getting the course into trim.

September 11.

It seems to me that two holes will be of critical importance, the tenth and the sixth. The freaky little tenth measures only 275 yards and is either a blah of a par-four, played with something like a six-iron followed by a pitch across a pond, or a white-knuckle three-shotter calling for a full wood to be directed through the narrowest air corridor in British golf. Deviate by a degree or so either side of that curving approach path and you find water, or trees, or sand or a flower bed. It is what our chaps call a bottle hole, the Americans a right mother.

The sixth is 396 yards played over a stream and a brow, which makes the tee shot partially blind. A full drive in still air would pitch between two substantial lakes. I measure this landing area at 40 yards. The fairway narrows at this point to a mere 18 yards and half of it slopes so steeply that a drive would kick away into the semi-rough. Obviously, the driver carries a quite unacceptable risk. Sure enough, all the players are going with irons off the tee. Sam Torrance, Howard Clark and Jose Rivero make a complete nonsense of the hole. With sinking heart I observe that Sandy Lyle is putting the ball into places from which only Sandy

Lyle could possibly recover, which bodes decidedly dodgy for the foursomes. Nick Faldo is also off his stick. I determine to stay out until I can find five Americans who are playing equally badly.

Fortunately it does not take me all that long to identify five candidates: Mark O'Meara, Hal Sutton, Fuzzy Zoeller, Andy North and Peter Jacobsen. Feeling better, I return to the tented press centre and devour a tepid Cornish pastie in the cafeteria. The coffee, however, is excellent and I immediately become addicted.

The American non-playing captain, Lee Trevino, is brought in for interview. These occasions are pretty pointless because they are purely exercises in psychological warfare. Trevino is a master of this kind of hype and presents a picture of relaxed confidence. The one solid fact he reveals is that he has laid down as a matter of team policy that his team must not indulge in heroics at the tenth in the foursomes. In the fourballs, the first player can have a pop at the green and if he succeeds then his partner can have a go. In the singles it will be at the discretion of each individual.

This phony war before the event starts is always tiresome but I am relieved to hear that Tony Jacklin is laying down no rules about how to play the tenth, on the grounds that his team are capable of making their own judgments. Captaincy will certainly play a major role in the outcome of the match and I put Jacklin one up.

I am glad that I am not staying in The Belfry when Jock Mac-Vicar, correspondent of the *Scottish Daily Express,* relates how he was stopped by a security guard on his way to the bathroom. Mac-Vicar produced his room key and his press credentials but it still took him five minute's of argument to establish his *bona fides.* He just made the bathroom in time.

I return to my regular farmhouse hotel and at the end of dinner I bite into a piece of Gorgonzola and encouter a lump of grit. A good gulp of house claret swills the offending loose impediment into oblivion. My probing tongue then discovers that a dental crown has become detached from its steel post and I have swallowed it. What a wonderful life!

September 12.

Drive into Lichfield in search of a dentist. At the first one I try the receptionist says that I can sit in the waiting room in case of a cancellation. With all the resignation I can muster I station myself within arm's length of a pile of old *National Geographic* magazines and settle down for a long wait. Halfway through an article on the mammals of Sumatra I am called. A saint in a white overall takes out a tray of Unipart teeth and within 20 minutes I am out in the street, plus a gleaming new incisor and minus £7.50. Just imagine what that would have set me back in Los Angeles.

In my mind this incident looms as a sort of portent, an early set-back which all comes right in the end.

It is another beautiful day and back at The Belfry the teams are having their final practice round. Trevino is making his men play real foursomes, as opposed to their usual habit of all driving off and then swapping balls for the next shot. He has put up 1,000 dollars for the pair with the lowest score. (Tom Kite and Calvin Peete copped for the loot with a 69).

On the course I come across Jacklin and Bernard Gallacher sitting on a golf cart and, despite the sunshine, wearing water-proof suits. I ask Jacklin if he is under the impression that it is pouring with rain. "No, I'm freezing my bollocks off," he replies, whatever that may mean. Possibly a Lincolnshire expression. Great hilarity in the press tent where a perplexed sub-editor of *The Standard* has been on the phone seeking an explanation for repeated references to Lee Elder in Renton Laidlaw's copy. As it happens *The Standard* has recently put out an advertisement with a picture of Laidlaw and the legend:

'EXCLUSIVE: Britain's Top Golf Writer writes for the London Standard.' *The caption read:* 'Not just a good writer, but not a bad golfer. Renton Laidlaw wins the Golf Writers' Autumn Medal Tournament in 1984'.

This ad is quickly photocopied, endorsed with cruel jibes and left on his typewriter. We are all guilty of aberrations from time to time but this was a classic and will doubtless go into the lore of the press tent.

The captains now exchange their pairings for the first series of foursomes in the morning and by general agreement Jacklin has assembled his strongest teams. At the flag raising ceremony the colour party manages to get the Union Jack the right way up, which makes a change after last week's European Masters in Switzerland, not to mention the U.S. Masters at Augusta.

September 13.

It all goes wrong, with a 3 – 1 points haul to the visitors. I sit down calmly and reassemble the arguments for a European victory.

One point margin in Florida two years ago, reform of team selection system, decline of U.S. superstars, Sandy Lyle's Open championship and Bernhard Langer's Masters victory finally dissolve the traditional European inferiority complexes, not to mention the Spanish domination of the World Cup and Severiano Ballesteros's domination of everything and everyone. No, it was going to be all right.

I decide not to be depressed . . . besides, I am engrossed in a professional problem which we literary types frequently encounter, namely how to describe Jacklin's face. It is grey and has a congealed look about it which is reminiscent of something from my past. That's it! Cold porridge. His nervous system has clearly taken a terrible pounding as he drove from match to match, anxiously enquiring on his walkie-talkie if there was any good news from the others.

Jacklin may have felt as if he had been kicked in the stomach by a horse but his reasoning faculties are still razor sharp. Trevino had made it clear that he did not propose to deviate from the normal American policy of giving all his players as many matches as possible. His winning partnership of Kite and Peete is rested for the afternoon fourballs. Jacklin is set on a ruthless policy of playing his strongest players as often as he can. That is not an easy decision for him because he has put his professional reputation on the line in selecting Faldo, Brown and Rivero. He leaves all three on the sidelines, since they have been out of form in practice, and also dumps Lyle. His tactics pay off by $2\frac{1}{2}$ points to $1\frac{1}{2}$ and a hint of colour returns to the cold porridge.

The American golf magazine, *Golf Digest,* for which I am an honoured contributor, call me in the evening on a subject unrelated to the Ryder Cup match. I ask if they would like me to write a few words about the stirring events at The Belfry when it is all over and they tell me that unfortunately they have no available space. Nothing is said, of course, but the implication is clear: yet another American victory in the Ryder Cup match ranks on a par with 'Man Does Not Bite Dog.'

September 14.

Torrance and Clark, who have come up blank from two tight matches on the first day, lead off the fourballs and reward Jacklin's faith in them by turning over Kite and North. Way and Woosnam, who both have to jump up and down in order to peep over the rim of their golf bags, cut Green and Zoeller down to size. The morning is looking like an even split when Langer and Lyle come to the last one down to Stadler and Strange. It is all over as Stadler steps up to put away the 18-inch putt which will secure the precious point and maintain America's overall lead in the match. The much vaunted British reputation for sportsmanship takes a dent as 25,000 voices roar with approval when he misses. At his midday interview Trevino is laid back about the affair, saying that these things happen and that the spirits of his men were unimpaired.

Jacklin agrees up to a point. These things do indeed happen in this funny game. But Jacklin insists that this mishap is of high significance, devastating to American morale whatever they might say, and heartening for his team.

During the break I run into John Jacobs, the previous nonplaying captain of the European team. We share a few reservations about Jacklin's pairings for that afternoon's second series of foursomes. Rivero is being given his Ryder Cup baptism, in partnership with Jose-Maria Canizares, and Langer is playing with his fourth partner of the match, Ken Brown. We agree that at this psychologically advantageous moment Jacklin should have stayed with the players who had been doing the business for Europe. Still, Stadler's missed putt has created a mood of euphoria which even survives a Henry Cotton joke about a golfer who falls on hard times and does a music hall act involving a six inch nail. I manage quite a convincing guffaw.

Soon Rivero and Canizares are producing the kind of golf which prompted Trevino to remark that his top pairing, Kite and Peete, had walked into a buzz saw. Jacklin's tactics are gloriously vindicated by a 3 – 1 swing, including a Ryder Cup record margin of 7 and 5 by the buzz saw boys, giving Europe a two point lead to take into the final series of 12 singles. The press tent statisticians go to work and come up with the information that this was the first time the Americans had trailed at this stage for 40 years. Or perhaps 50. Absolute yonks, anyway.

Dinner is again disturbed by a telephone call, this time from the stern editor of a Scottish Sunday newspaper demanding that his correspondent rewrite his copy and explain why he had forecast an American victory. What a wonderful life!

September 15.

Trevino is still as bouncy as ever. He explains that he has put his strongest players at the head of the field in order to wipe out the two point deficit and put heart into the others. This move is inevitable and Jacklin has anticipated it, packing his strength in the middle of the order. After all, he needs only five and a half points and feels that the best way to get them is to send his storm troopers in against the soft underbelly of the American team.

According to this plan, Manuel Pinero must be seen as a sacrificial lamb. He is drawn against Lanny Wadkins, the undoubted hero of the American side.

Wadkins has played some terrific golf, as usual, and he is one of the toughest match-players you could hope to meet. There is so much bull terrier in the Wadkins bloodline that you would not be surprised if he chewed up your slippers. It says everything for the spirit in the European camp that when Jacklin announces the pairings Pinero jumps up and says: "He is exactly the one I wanted".

There is no gamer battler in all Europe than the tiny Pinero and in just over two hours' time I am congratulating him on taking Wadkins apart. As always, Pinero is modest and quietly spoken and he remarks, assuredly meaning it as a compliment, that he believes Wadkins to be one of the few Americans who could earn a living on the European Tour. The wind, he explains, would destroy the swings of most of them.

So the sacrificial lamb has devoured the executioner and that is the first bonus for Europe. Then Way beats America's most experienced campaigner in Raymond Floyd and Ballesteros holds Kite to a half. Trevino's master plan is in tatters, comprehensively so as Lyle takes Jacobsen by three and two. Sutton's resistance collapses against the unrelenting Langer and the European impetus is irresistible. It is just a matter of time, and of who will be the player to claim the decisive point.

I suppose that objectively we have to say that the decisive point was won when the dispirited North drove into the pond at the 18th. The rest is formality but Torrance completes the formalities in grand style with a birdie.

Tony Jacklin comes storming into the tent and grabs me in a bear hug, exulting: "They did it. They bloody did it". I correct him: "You did it" for I truly believe that this is in large measure Jacklin's victory. Ken Schofield, Executive Director of the European Tour, pumps me by the hand in delight and to him too must go a big slice of the credit. After all, he created the proving ground for world class players.

The margin of victory is not too relevant on these occasions because once the winning point is on the board then the incomplete matches are strictly for the record books. Still, five clear points may make the American golf public sit up and take notice and guarantee a gate at Muirfield Village, Ohio, in 1987.

I drive home to learn that the tribe has increased by the addition of a girl child. Never mind. A double celebration is in order. My wife scotches that idea by telling me of an urgent message from *Golf Digest*. They want a long piece on the Ryder Cup match and are holding the magazine open to accommodate my immediate telephoned copy. Never mind. What a wonderful life!

8 *The Future*
by Michael McDonnell

History may well recall that the balance of power in world golf changed irrevocably at the precise moment Sam Torrance sank the winning putt. The truth however is somewhat different.

Of itself, The Ryder Cup triumph might have meant nothing more than an aberration in the run of form; the inevitable defeat that waits in ambush for any supremely successful side; and the nightmare that haunted every American captain.

That certainly had been the case back in 1957 at Lindrick when, completely against the form book and expectations of the home side, the Americans had been defeated. Yet when the match was over and the cheering had stopped, nothing really had changed. Nobody doubted that the Americans were still the best golfers in the world.

Indeed the success of the British and Irish team did not prompt a huge public discovery of golf nor lure thousands of youngsters to foresake their cricket bats and footballs and head for the first tee.

The whole affair had been nothing more than a minor upset that admittedly left warm and proud memories among the victors yet held no greater significance other than confirmation of the giant-killing axiom that "on the day" anybody can be beaten.

But what happened at The Belfry was different. It was the effect – the culmination perhaps – of a revolution that had been taking place in European golf for a decade or more; indeed since

Tony Jacklin burst upon the scene in 1969 to capture the Open championship and demonstrate that golf was a young man's game – and that of a rich young man too.

Thus any study of where Ryder Cup success will now lead must first dwell on the past and consider the developments within the game that have set the pattern which has brought about the most successful year in the history of European golf.

And it is in this context that the Ryder Cup triumph must be considered. It is but part of a thrilling European resurgence that has seen a Spaniard acknowledged as the greatest golfer in the world, a German snapping up the American Masters title from the best the US Tour could offer and a British professional capturing the Open championship that hitherto dwarfed and suffocated home players by its sheer magnitude.

Against such a background it is not too hard to guess the mood of confidence that permeated the European side when it assembled at The Belfry; when even the more junior members of the team could see they were standing shoulder-to-shoulder with the world's most successful golfers in the current order.

Such evidence, after all, rubbed off on the British and Irish side back in 1969 at Royal Birkdale when the home team beheld the newly-crowned Open champion Tony Jacklin in their midst offering living proof that Americans really were beatable and thereby inspiring a classic and historic tied match.

How then did the great European revival begin? And on what course had it been set? More importantly, can it now transform golf into a mass appeal sport, particularly in continental countries where the game has been pursued by the very rich who played it and the very poor who caddied for it and sometimes became professionals at it?

My own view is that the revival began with Tony Jacklin who was himself as much part of the vibrancy and fresh endeavour of the Swinging Sixties as The Beatles and the Rolling Stones. Just as they threw off old values and precepts so too did Jacklin, in his world, lay to rest old traditions and superstitions especially ones about invincible Americans.

What happened then was that golf broadened its appeal among the young. It was taught in schools and reached an audience that had no previous awareness or connection with the game. Nick Faldo is an excellent example of a great talent coming into the game with no known pedigree to his name. He first saw the game while watching television and decided he would like to try it.

When Jacklin was winning at Royal Lytham in 1969, the likes

of Nick Faldo, Bernhard Langer, Sandy Lyle and Severiano Ballesteros were 12 years old. For them, there was much developing to be done before they could stand alongside his achievements. Indeed during the doldrums of the mid-Seventies when nobody of significance emerged to challenge Jacklin, the constant cry after every Ryder Cup defeat and Open failure was: "What's wrong with our golf?"

The chorus was loudest after every Ryder Cup match because somehow this was the biennial reminder of inferiority; the testimony to on-going inadequacy. Even Tony Jacklin's triumph was double-edged because he had learned the champion's craft on the U.S. Tour and there were those who argued that until Europe itself produced a champion from its own tour, its value would always be open to question.

How sweet therefore that it should now have produced two, possibly three – in Ballesteros, Lyle and Langer – and that many more are poised to follow that pattern.

The fact is that during the quiescent period of the Seventies a lot was happening that shaped the future of the game. Those of us on the circuit who saw the raw talent were encouraged by its depth and volume, but also knew it would emerge in its own good time. True enough, we newspaper writers still joined the chorus of gloom although curiously that in itself was to have a positive effect because it forced PGA officials to open up Ryder Cup team membership to continental golfers, primarily to enlist the services of Ballesteros, to make a match of it.

In any case, that was a logical move since the major European golf countries – France, Germany, Spain, Italy, Portugal, Holland, Sweden – were part of the professional circuit; a legacy from the inspired decision by the then tour boss John Jacobs to broaden the circuit because of the limitations within the British Isles.

The effect of this continental tour with its widely differing types of golf course, climate, food, language and customs was to produce players of unprecedented durability, with both technique and confidence to deal with the lushness of La Manga in Spain one week then switch without missing a stride to the chilling terrain of Turnberry the next.

Moreover, global travel itself became an integral part of the way of life for these professionals as they toured Africa, the Far East, Australia and made the occasional sortie to the United States.

Thus were all these differing strands and influences coming together with one inevitable conclusion – to produce European golfers of supreme class.

147

Even before the great success of '85, the signs were obvious. Nick Faldo took the 1984 Sea Pines Heritage Classic, at Hilton Head, one of the toughest courses on the U.S. circuit against one of its strongest fields.

Sandy Lyle took one of the richest prizes in U.S. golf when he won the Kapalua International in Hawaii in 1984. And before that Sam Torrance had narrowly lost a play-off for the Southern Open.

The old fears about American supremacy were on the wane. And that was made unequivocally apparent by the manner in which the European professionals sprang eagerly to the attack from the very start of the Ryder Cup encounter at The Belfry, never relaxing until the battle was won.

The implications of that historic moment take many forms, the most important of which is the presentation of a new image of golf to a public that assumed the game possessed neither pace nor excitement.

During the three days of the Belfry contest, televised golf reached a gigantic new audience. Such was the drama of the occasion, perhaps too a British love of team involvement, that televised golf broke free from its specialist-viewing category and actually appeared in the ratings in company with soap operas, comedy programmes and other mass appeal offerings.

People who had never played the game became entranced by it and caught up in its excitement as a home team – yes, even the Spaniards and the German – were cheered to victory.

It was, too, a refreshing spectacle after a depressing saga of death and destruction surrounding professional sport earlier in the year, to see these golfers playing as best they could, not for money (because no fee was involved) but for the glory. (Of course, there was the eventual prospect of greater prize money if European golf elevated its status by such success but that was not the thought uppermost in the minds of those players who wore the team colours that week).

What happened at The Belfry was that the game at long last lost its mysteries to a public who had assumed the sport was too profound, too selective, too difficult and too expensive for the likes of them.

The most important era in the history of golf was about to dawn not just in public participation but in a more general awareness that would make the sport itself the perfect vehicle for commercial promotion and advertising on which sport sponsorship is based.

While more schools are now asking the Golf Foundation to

provide lessons for golf-minded kids; while the queues at public courses grow longer because the development of new links has not keep pace, it is behind the scenes that the Ryder Cup success is likely to have the most significant effect on the future of the game.

Again, it is necessary to study the past to discover the reasons. For years, professional golf in Europe – particularly in Britain – had been a buyer's market. It rested largely in the control of sponsors and entrepreneurs who called the tune.

Their task was to present their products in the best possible image and because of the absence of top quality golf stars in Britain and Europe, this obviously meant hiring the best from the United States, generally for huge fees, while not paying too much heed to the disapproving growls of the Professional Golfers Association whose rank-and-file were picking up whatever money the superstars left.

An unsatisfactory state of affairs, but really one that could not be changed until the European tour strengthened its bargaining power by possessing its own world-class stars who would pledge their support. Tony Jacklin at his peak had played his part but as his playing influence diminished in the mid-seventies, so did his demand.

In fairness to the entrepreneurs, their style had enormous benefits in getting golf itself established in countries where there was virtually no history of the sport. The mass appeal of golf in Sweden for example began less than 20 years ago with an exhibition match between Jack Nicklaus and ex-ice hockey star Sven Tumba.

Yet now it has reached the proportions and stature of a national past-time – and this in a country that is under snow for many months of the year. Even so, the Swedes with astonishing fervour, practice indoors waiting for the snows to melt. With the kind of methodical efficiency that produced their tennis stars, they have now set about making golf stars and Tony Jacklin sees them as a dominant force in any future Ryder Cup side.

What happened therefore at The Belfry changed the power behind-the-scenes in a way that neither Sandy Lyle's Open triumph, Bernhard Langer's Masters victory nor Severiano's undisputed class could manage. All had been priceless boosts to the stature of the game but, for all that, evidence particularly of their own flair and ability.

But it was the collective force and triumph of European golfers in the Ryder Cup that confirmed their general importance and put the governing power of the game where it belonged, in the hands of the European tour officials and the players themselves.

The shift of power. Ben Crenshaw hands over the Masters Green Jacket to
Bernhard Langer

This is what Jacklin meant when he said the Ryder Cup men were playing for their own future and prize money for years to come.

There is now no doubt that the European tour can provide all the star material any sponsor desires. In truth, a dozen men may have triumphed at The Belfry but the best part of another dozen could have filled the lower orders of that team without any detrimental effect on the outcome.

In the hysteria that followed Torrance's winning putt, one senior professional turned to Executive Director Ken Schofield and said: "If you can't get a circuit worth £20 million a year, then I don't know." Understandable jubilation, but not really thought through to a realistic conclusion.

True enough, the prospects of European golf are attractive enough to persuade Severiano to reduce his commitment to the U.S. tour. Sandy Lyle has also made it clear he is quite happy to stay within easy reach of home and not race round the world, a hurtful mistake others have made at savage cost to their careers. Lyle said quite wisely: "After all, how much money does one man need?"

Yet the weakness of the prophecy about untold riches for golf is that even if there were a clamour of new sponsors offering huge sums to get on the band wagon, the sport has too many painful experiences of "sky's-the-limit" sponsors who disappear as suddenly as they arrive.

Schofield himself has always adopted a cautious approach to spectacular offers preferring instead to assure long term benefits for the game which is one reason why he has not held television companies to ransom during the revival of European golf, being content to take low fees for more TV coverage so that more sponsors will finance tournament golf and in the knock-on process permit more young professionals to play and improve.

But all the unprecedented success has presented European golfers with a dilemma. Is the circuit still just the stepping stone to bigger things? If so, then will the emerging stars move on to the U.S. tour as they have always done? Or can it now stand in its own right as the legitimate ambition for any world class golfer? Would Americans, for example, see it as a world to conquer? Or would they rather stay home? Is an Irish Open as prestigious as a Western Open or a Los Angeles Open?

For certain, the Ryder Cup success and the individual victories of tour members will themselves prompt more success from other players if only because of the old belief that "anything you can do, I can do etc". Winning the Open is not a dream. Sandy Lyle proved that. So, too, did Severiano Ballesteros.

That puts it within the realistic range of a legion of young professionals who themselves on a given day can beat Sandy and Sevvy. Just as the Ryder Cup will now travel backwards and forwards across the Atlantic between teams of like standards, so too will the Open no longer remain the monopoly of a precious few but is certain to bear many more European names.

Ryder Cup success should also prompt the Americans to open their doors to more players if only to add sparkle to their own lacklustre tour which is filled with look-alike winners, none of whom make the kind of personal impact the game needs to survive.

That, after all, is no more than the European professionals – for all they have done in the world – are due. But if that happens in volume then the European tour itself will be depleted, and perhaps lose that vital bargaining power. Such men are world heroes and are deservedly in demand. Yet the same loyalty that made them play their hearts out for victory, is still required to assure the future of a tour that made it all possible.

9 *Complete Results*

Great Britain v. U.S.A. (Professionals)

At Gleneagles, Perthshire, June 6th, 1921

SINGLES

GREAT BRITAIN	Matches	U.S.A.	Matches
G. Duncan (2 and 1)	1	J. Hutchison	0
A. Mitchell (halved)	0	W. Hagen (halved)	0
E. Ray	0	E. French (2 and 1)	1
J. H. Taylor	0	F. McLeod (1 hole)	1
H. Vardon (3 and 1)	1	T. Kerrigan	0
J. Braid (5 and 4)	1	C. Hackney	0
A. Havers	0	W. Reid (2 and 1)	1
J. Ockenden (5 and 4)	1	G. McLean	0
J. Sherlock (3 and 2)	1	C. Hoffner	0
Josh Taylor (3 and 2)	1	W. Mehlhorn	0
	—		—
	6		3

FOURSOMES

GREAT BRITAIN	Matches	USA	Matches
G. Duncan and A. Mitchell (halved)	0	J. Hutchison and W. Hagen (halved)	0
E. Ray and H. Vardon (5 and 4)	1	E. French and T. Kerrigan	0
J. Braid and J. H. Taylor (halved)	0	C. Hackney and F. McLeod (halved)	0
A. Havers and J. Ockenden (6 and 5)	1	W. Reid and J. McLean	0
J. Sherlock and Josh Taylor (1 hole)	1	C. Hoffner and W. Mehlhorn	0
	—		—
	3		0

Grand Aggregate: Great Britain, 9; U.S.A., 3 (3 matches halved).

At Wentworth, June 4th and 5th, 1926.

SINGLES

GREAT BRITAIN	Matches	U.S.A.	Matches
Abe Mitchell (8 and 7)	1	Jim Barnes	0
George Duncan (6 and 5)	1	Walter Hagen	0
Aubrey Boomer (2 and 1)	1	Thos Armour	0
A. Compston	0	W. Melhorn (1 hole)	1
George Gadd (8 and 7)	1	Joe Kirkwood	0
E. Ray	1	Al Watrous	0
Fred Robson (5 and 4)	1	Cyril Walker	0
Arthur Havers (10 and 9)	1	Fred McLeod	0
E. R. Whitcombe (halved)	0	Emmett French (halved)	0
H. C. Jolly (3 and 2)	1	Joe Stein	0
	—		—
	8		1

FOURSOMES

GREAT BRITAIN	Matches	U.S.A.	Matches
Abe Mitchell and George Duncan (9 and 8)	1	Jim Barnes and Walter Hagen	0
Aubrey Boomer and Archie Compston (3 and 2)	1	T. Armour and Joe Kirkwood	0
George Gadd and Arthur Havers (3 and 2)	1	W. Melhorn and Al Watrous	0
E. Ray and Fred Robson (3 and 2)	1	Cyril Walker and Fred McLeod	0
E. R. Whitcombe and H. C. Jolly (3 and 2)	1	Emmett French and Joe Stein	0
	—		—
	5		0

Grand Aggregate: Great Britain, 13; U.S.A., 1; 1 match halved.

Ryder Cup

At Worcester, Mass., U.S.A., June 3rd and 4th, 1927.

FOURSOMES

U.S.A.	Matches	GREAT BRITAIN	Matches
W. Hagen and J. Golden (2 and 2)	1	E. Ray and F. Robson	0
J. Farrell and J. Turnesa (8 and 6)	1	G. Duncan and A. Compston	0
E. Sarazen and A. Watrous (3 and 2)	1	A. Havers and H. Jolly	0
L. Diegel and W. Melhorn	0	A. Boomer and C. A. Whitcombe (7 and 5)	1
	3		1

SINGLES

U.S.A.	Matches	GREAT BRITAIN	Matches
W. Melhorn, Westmorland (1 hole)	1	A. Compston, Wolverhampton	0
J. Farrell, Quaker Ridge (5 and 4)	1	A. Boomer, St. Cloud, Paris	0
J. Golden, N. Jersey (8 and 7)	1	H. C. Jolly, Foxgrove	0
L. Diegel, Glen Oaks (7 and 5)	1	E. Ray, Oxhey	0
E. Sarazen, Fresh Meadow (halved)	0	C. A. Whitcombe, Crews Hill (halved)	0
W. Hagen, Detroit (2 and 1)	1	A. G. Havers, Coombe Hill	0
A. Watrous, Grand Rapids (3 and 2)	1	F. Robson, Cooden Beach	0
J. Turnesa, Fair View	0	G. Duncan, Wentworth (1 hole)	1
	6		1

Grand Aggregate: U.S.A., 9 matches; Great Britain, 2 matches; 1 match halved.
Captains: Edward Ray, Great Britain, and Walter Hagen, U.S.A.

At Moortown, Leeds, May 26th and 27th, 1929.

FOURSOMES

U.S.A.	Matches	GREAT BRITAIN	Matches
J. Farrell and J. Turnesa	0	C. A. Whitcombe and A. Compston (halved)	0
L. Diegel and A. Espinosa (7 and 5)	1	A Boomer and G. Duncan	0
E. Sarazen and E. Dudley	0	A. Mitchell and F. Robson (2 and 1)	1
J. Golden and W. Hagen (2 up)	1	E. R. Whitcombe and T. H. Cotton	0
	2		1

SINGLES

U.S.A.	Matches	GREAT BRITAIN	Matches
J. Farrell	0	C. A. Whitcombe (8 and 6)	1
W. Hagen	0	G. Duncan (10 and 8)	1
L. Diegel (9 and 8)	1	A. Mitchell	0
E. Sarazen	0	A. Compston (6 and 4)	1
J. Turnesa	0	A. Boomer (4 and 3)	1
Horton Smith (4 and 2)	1	Fred Robson	0
Al Watrous	0	T. H. Cotton (4 and 3)	1
A. Espinosa (halved)	0	E. R. Whitcombe (halved)	0
	2		5

Grand Aggregate: Great Britain, 6 matches; U.S.A., 4 matches; 2 matches halved.
Captains: George Duncan, Great Britain, and W. Hagen, U.S.A.

At Scioto, Columbus, Ohio, U.S.A., June 26th and 27th, 1931.

FOURSOMES

GREAT BRITAIN	Matches	U.S.A.	Matches
Archie Compston and W. H. Davies	0	E. Sarazen and Johnny Farrell (8 and 7)	1
George Duncan and Arthur Havers	0	Walter Hagen and Densmore Shute (10 and 9)	1
Abe Mitchell and Fred Robson (3 and 1)	1	Leo Diegel and Al Espinosa	0
Syd Easterbrook and Ernest Whitcombe	0	Billy Burke and "Whiffy" Cox (3 and 2)	1
	1		3

SINGLES

GREAT BRITAIN	Matches	U.S.A.	Matches
Archie Compston	0	Billy Burke (7 and 6)	1
Fred Robson	0	E. Sarazen (7 and 6)	1

GREAT BRITAIN	Matches	U.S.A.	Matches
W. H. Davies (4 and 3)	1	Johnny Farrell	0
Abe Mitchell	0	"Whiffy" Cox (3 and 1)	1
C. A. Whitcombe	0	Walter Hagen (4 and 3)	1
Bert Hodson	0	Densmore Shute (8 and 6)	1
E. Whitcombe	0	Al Espinosa (2 and 1)	1
Arthur Havers (4 and 3)	1	C. Wood	0
	2		6

Grand Aggregate: U.S.A., 9 matches; Great Britain, 3 matches.
Captions: C. A. Whitcombe, Great Britain, and W. Hagen, U.S.A..

At Southport and Ainsdale Course, Southport, June 26th and 27th, 1933.

FOURSOMES

GREAT BRITAIN	Matches	U.S.A.	Matches
Percy Alliss and C. A. Whitcombe (halved)	0	E. Sarazen and Walter Hagen (halved)	0
Abe Mitchell and Arthur Havers (3 and 2)	1	Olin Dutra and Densmore Shute	0
W. H. Davies and S. Easterbrook (1 up)	1	Craig Wood and Paul Runyan	0
A. H. Padgham and A. Perry	0	Ed. Dudley and Billy Burke (1 up)	1
	2		1

SINGLES

GREAT BRITAIN	Matches	U.S.A.	Matches
A. H. Padgham	0	E. Sarazen (6 and 4)	1
Abe Mitchell (9 and 8)	1	Olin Dutra	0
A. J. Lacey	0	Walter Hagen (2 and 1)	1
W. H. Davies	0	Craig Wood (4 and 3)	1
Percy Alliss (2 and 1)	1	Paul Runyan	0
Arthur Havers (4 and 3)	1	Leo Diegel	0
Syd Easterbrook (1 hole)	1	Densmore Shute	0
C. A. Whitcombe	0	Horton Smith (2 and 1)	1
	4		4

Grand Aggregates: Great Britain, 6 matches; U.S.A., 5 matches; 1 match halved.
Captains: J. H. Taylor, Great Britain (non-playing), and W. Hagen, U.S.A.

At Ridgewood, New Jersey, September 28th and 29th, 1935.

FOURSOMES

U.S.A.	Matches	GREAT BRITAIN	Matches
E. Sarazen (unattached) and W. Hagen (unattached) (7 and 6)	1	A. Perry (Leatherhead) and J. E. Busson (Pannal)	0
H. Picard (Hershey and Milwaukee) and J. Revolta (Tripoli) (6 and 5)	1	A. H. Padgham (Sundridge Park) and P. Alliss (Beaconsfield)	0
Paul Runyan (Metropolitan) and Horton Smith (Oak Park, Ill) (9 and 8)	1	W. J. Cox (Addington) and E. W. Jarman (Prenton)	0
Olin Dutra (Wiltshire, Los Angeles) Ky. Laffoon (Northmoor, Ill.)	0	C. A. Whitcombe (Crews Hill) and E. R. Whitcombe (Meyrick Park) (1 hole)	1
	3		1

SINGLES

U.S.A.	Matches	GREAT BRITAIN	Matches
E. Sarazen (3 and 2)	1	Busson	0
P. Runyan (5 and 3)	1	Burton	0
J. Revolta (2 and 1)	1	R. Whitcombe	0
O. Dutra (4 and 2)	1	Padgham	0
Craig Wood	0	Alliss (1 hole)	1
Horton Smith (halved)	0	Cox (halved)	0
H. Picard (3 and 2)	1	E. Whitcombe	0
S. Parks (halved)	0	Perry (halved)	0
	5		1

Grand Aggregates: U.S.A., 8 matches; Great Britain, 2 matches; 2 matches halved.
Captains: C. A. Whitcombe, Great Britain, and W. Hagen, U.S.A.

At Southport and Ainsdale, June 29th and 30th, 1937.

FOURSOMES

GREAT BRITAIN	Matches	U.S.A.	Matches
A. H. Padgham (Sundridge Park) and T. H. Cotton (Ashridge)	0	Ed. Dudley (Philadelphia) and Byron Nelson (Ridgewood) (4 and 2)	1
A. J. Lacey (Berkshire) and W. J. Cox (Wimbledon Park)	0	R. Guldahl (Beverley Hills) and Tony Manero (Greensborough) (2 and 1)	1
C. A. Whitcombe (Crews Hill) and D. J. Rees (Surbiton) (halved)		E. Sarazen (Brookfield) and D. Shute (West Newton) (halved)	0
P. Alliss (Templenewsam) and R. Burton (Hooton) (2 and 1)	1	H. Picard (Hershey, Penn.) and J. Revolta (Niles Centre)	0
	1		2

SINGLES

GREAT BRITAIN	Matches	U.S.A.	Matches
A. H. Padgham	0	R. Guldahl (8 and 7)	1
S. L. King (halved)	0	D. Shute (halved)	0
D. J. Rees (3 and 1)	1	B. Nelson	0
T. H. Cotton (5 and 3)	1	T. Manero	0
P. Alliss	0	E. Sarazen (1 hole)	1
R. Burton	0	S. Snead (5 and 4)	1
A. Perry	0	E. Dudley (2 and 1)	1
A. J. Lacey	0	H. Picard (2 and 1)	1
	2		5

Grand Aggregates: U.S.A., 7 matches; Great Britain, 3 matches; 2 matches halved.
Captains: C. A. Whitcombe, Great Britain, and W. Hagen, U.S.A. (non-playing).

1939 – Due to be played at Ponte Vedra, Jacksonville, November 18th-19th, 1939. No contest owing to European War.

British Players chosen for 1939 were: – T. H. Cotton (captain), R. Burton, R. A. Whitcombe, S. L. King, A. H. Padgham, C. A. Whitcombe, D. J. Rees, J. Adams. Selection of two more players had been deferred. The U.S. team chosen for 1939 was: – Vic Ghezzi, R. Guldahl, J. Hines, H. McSpaden, Dick Metz, H. Picard, Paul Runyan, Horton Smith and Sam Snead, with W. Hagen as non-playing Captain.

In 1941 the U.S. again chose a team comprising: J. Demaret, Vic Ghezzi, Ben Hogan, H. McSpaden, Lloyd Mangrum, Byron Nelson, Gene Sarazen, Horton Smith, Sam Snead, and Craig Wood, with W. Hagen as non-playing captain.

At Portland, Oregon, November 1st and 2nd, 1947.

FOURSOMES

U.S.A.	Matches	GREAT BRITAIN	Matches
Ed. Oliver and Lew Worsham (10 and 9)	1	T. H. Cotton and A. Lees	0
S. Snead and L. Mangrum (6 and 5)	1	F. Daly and C. H. Ward	0
B. Hogan and J. Demaret (2 holes)	1	J. Adams and M. Faulkner	0
Byron Nelson and H. Barron (2 and 1)	1	D. J. Rees and S. King	0
	4		0

SINGLES

U.S.A.	Matches	GREAT BRITAIN	Matches
E. J. Harrison (5 and 4)	1	F. Daly	0
L. Worsham (3 and 2)	1	J. Adams	0
L. Mangrum (6 and 5)	1	M. Faulkner	0
Ed. Oliver (4 and 3)	1	C. H. Ward	0
Byron Nelson (2 and 1)	1	A. Lees	0
S. Snead (5 and 4)	1	T. H. Cotton	0
J. Demaret (3 and 2)	1	D. J. Rees	0
H. Kelser	0	S. King (4 and 3)	1
	7		1

Grand Aggregates: U.S.A., 11 matches; Great Britain, 1 match.
Captains: T. Henry Cotton, Great Britain, and Ben Hogan, U.S.A.

At Ganton, Scarborough, September 16th and 17th, 1949.

FOURSOMES

GREAT BRITAIN	Matches	U.S.A.	Matches
M. Faulkner and J. Adams (2 and 1)	1	E. J. Harrison and J. Palmer	0
F. Daly and K. Bousfield (4 and 2)	1	R. Hamilton and S. Alexander	0
C. Ward and S. L. King	0	J. Demaret and C. Heafner (4 and 3)	1

R. Burton and A. Lees (1 hole)	1	S. Snead and L. Mangrum	0
	3		1

SINGLES

GREAT BRITAIN	Matches	U.S.A.	Matches
M. Faulkner	0	E. J. Harrison (8 and 7)	1
J. Adams (2 and 1)	1	J. Palmer	0
C. Ward	0	S. Snead (6 and 5)	1
D. J. Rees (6 and 4)	1	R. Hamilton	0
R. Burton	0	C. Heafner (3 and 2)	1
S. King	0	C. Harbert (4 and 3)	1
A. Lees	0	J. Demaret (7 and 6)	1
F. Daly	0	L. Mangrum (1 hole)	1
	2		6

Grand Aggregates: U.S.A., 7 matches; Great Britain, 5 matches.
Captains (non playing): C. A. Whitcombe, Great Britain, and Ben Hogan, U.S.A.

At Pinehurst, North Carolina, November 2nd and 4th, 1951.

FOURSOMES

U.S.A.	Matches	GREAT BRITAIN	Matches
C. Heafner and J. Burke (5 and 3)	1	M. Faulkner and D. J. Rees	0
E. Oliver and H. Ransom	0	C. H. Ward and A. Lees (2 and 1)	1
L. Mangrum and S. Snead (5 and 4)	1	J. Adams and J. Panton	0
B. Hogan and J. Demaret (5 and 4)	1	F. Daly and K. Bousfield	0
	3		1

SINGLES

U.S.A.	Matches	GREAT BRITAIN	Matches
J. Burke (4 and 3)	1	J. Adams	0
J. Demaret (2 holes)	1	D. J. Rees	0
C. Heafner (halved)	0	F. Daly (halved)	0
L. Mangrum (6 and 5)	1	H. Weetman	0
E. Oliver	0	A. Lees (2 and 1)	1
B. Hogan (3 and 2)	1	C. H. Ward	0
S. Alexander (8 and 7)	1	J. Panton	0
S. Snead (4 and 3)	1	M. Faulkner	0
	6		1

Grand Aggregates: U.S.A., 9 matches; Great Britain, 2 matches; 1 match halved.
Captains: A. J. Lacey, Great Britain (non-playing) and Sam Snead, U.S.A.

At Wentworth, Surrey, October 2nd and 3rd, 1953.

FOURSOMES

GREAT BRITAIN	Matches	U.S.A.	Matches
H. Weetman and P. Alliss	0	D. Douglas and E. Oliver (2 and 1)	1
E. C. Brown and J. Panton	0	L. Mangrum and S. Snead (8 and 7)	1
J. Adams and B. J. Hunt	0	T. Kroll and J. Burke (7 and 5)	1
F. Daly and H. Bradshaw (1 hole)	1	W. Burkemo and C. Middlecoff	0
	1		3

SINGLES

GREAT BRITAIN	Matches	U.S.A.	Matches
D. J. Rees	0	J. Burke (2 and 1)	1
F. Daly (9 and 7)	1	T. Kroll	0
E. C. Brown (2 up)	1	L. Mangrum	0
H. Weetman (1 up)	1	S. Snead	0
M. Faulkner	0	C. Middlecoff (3 and 2)	1
P. Alliss	0	J. Turnesa (1 up)	1
B. J. Hunt (halved)	0	D. Douglas (halved)	0
H. Bradshaw (3 and 2)	1	F. Haas	0
	4		3

Grand Aggregates: U.S.A., 6 matches; Great Britain, 5 matches; 1 match halved.
Captains: T. H. Cotton, Great Britain (non-playing) and Lloyd Mangrum, U.S.A.

At Palm Springs, November 5th and 6th, 1955.

FOURSOMES

U.S.A.	Matches	GREAT BRITAIN	Matches
C. Harbert and J. Barber	0	J. Fallon and J. R. Jacobs (1 hole)	1
D. Ford and T. Kroll (5 and 4)	1	E. C. Brown and S. S. Scott	0
J. Burke and T. Bolt (1 hole)	1	A. Lees and H. Weetman	0
S. Snead and C. Middlecoff (3 and 2)	1	D. J. Rees and H. Bradshaw	0
	—		—
	3		1

SINGLES

U.S.A.	Matches	GREAT BRITAIN	Matches
T. Bolt (4 and 2)	1	C. O'Connor	0
C. Harbert (3 and 2)	1	S. S. Scott	0
C. Middlecoff	0	J. Jacobs (1 hole)	1
S. Snead (3 and 1)	1	D. J. Rees	0
M. Furgol	0	A. Lees (3 and 1)	1
J. Barber	0	E. C. Brown (3 and 2)	1
J. Burke (3 and 2)	1	H. Bradshaw	0
D. Ford (3 and 2)	1	H. Weetman	0
	—		—
	5		3

Grand Aggregates: U.S.A., 8 matches; Great Britain, 4 matches.
Captains: D.J. Rees, Great Britain, and Chick Harbert, U.S.A.

At Lindrick, Sheffield, October 4th and 5th, 1957.

FOURSOMES

GREAT BRITAIN	Matches	U.S.A.	Matches
P. Alliss and B. J. Hunt	0	D. Ford and D. Finsterwald (2 and 1)	1
K. Bousfield and D. J. Rees (3 and 2)	1	A. Wall and F. Hawkins	0
M. Faulkner and H. Weetman	0	T. Kroll and J. Burke (4 and 3)	1
C. O'Connor and E. C. Brown	0	R. Mayer and T. Bolt (7 and 5)	1
	—		—
	1		3

SINGLES

GREAT BRITAIN	Matches	U.S.A.	Matches
E. C. Brown (4 and 3)	1	T. Bolt	0
R. P. Mills (5 and 3)	1	J. Burke	0
P. Alliss	0	F. Hawkins (2 and 1)	1
K. Bousfield (4 and 3)	1	L. Hebert	0
D. J. Rees (7 and 6)	1	E. Furgol	0
B. J. Hunt (6 and 5)	1	D. Ford	0
C. O'Connor (7 and 6)	1	D. Finsterwald	0
H. Bradshaw (halved)	0	R. Mayer (halved)	0
	—		—
	6		1

Grand Aggregates: Great Britain, 7 matches; U.S.A., 4 matches; 1 match halved.
Captains: D. J. Rees, Great Britain, and Jack Burke, U.S.A.

At Palm Desert, California, November 6th and 7th, 1959.

FOURSOMES

U.S.A.	Matches	GREAT BRITAIN	Matches
R. Rosburg and M. Souchak (5 and 4)	1	B. J. Hunt and E. C. Brown	0
D. Ford and A. Wall	0	C. O'Connor and P. Alliss (3 and 2)	1
J. Boros and D. Finsterwald (2 holes)	1	D. J. Rees and K. Bousfield	0
S. Snead and C. Middlecoff (halved)	0	H. Weetman and D. C. Thomas (halved)	0
	—		—
	2		1

SINGLES

U.S.A.	Matches	GREAT BRITAIN	Matches
D. Ford (halved)	0	N. V. Drew (halved)	0
M. Souchak (3 and 2)	1	K. Bousfield	0
R. Rosburg (6 and 5)	1	H. Weetman	0
S. Snead (6 and 5)	1	D. C. Thomas	0
D. Finsterwald (1 hole)	1	D. J. Rees	0
J. Hebert (halved)	0	P. Alliss (halved)	0
A. Wall (7 and 6)	1	C. O'Connor	0
C. Middlecoff	0	E. C. Brown (4 and 3)	1
	—		—
	5		1

Grand Aggregates: U.S.A., 7 matches; Great Britain, 2 matches, with 3 matches halved.
Captains: D. J. Rees, Great Britain, and Sam Snead, U.S.A.

At Royal Lytham and St. Annes, October 13th and 14th, 1961.

FOURSOMES
Morning

GREAT BRITAIN	Matches	U.S.A.	Matches
C. O'Connor and P. Alliss (4 and 3)	1	G. Little and D. Ford	0
J. Panton and B. J. Hunt	0	A. Wall and J. Hebert (4 and 3)	1
D. J. Rees and K. Bousfield	0	W. Casper and A. Palmer (2 and 1)	1
T. B. Haliburton and N. C. Coles	0	M. Souchak and W. Collins (1 hole)	1

Afternoon

	Matches		Matches
C. O'Connor and P. Alliss	0	A. Wall and J. Hebert (1 hole)	1
J. Panton and B. J. Hunt	0	W. Casper and A. Palmer (5 and 4)	1
D. J. Rees and K. Bousfield (4 and 2)	1	M. Souchak and W. Collins	0
T. B. Haliburton and N. C. Coles	0	J. Barber and D. Finsterwald (1 hole)	1
	—		—
	2		6

SINGLES
Morning

GREAT BRITAIN	Matches	U.S.A.	Matches
H. Weetman	0	D. Ford (1 hole)	1
R. L. Moffitt	0	M. Souchak (5 and 4)	1
P. Alliss (halved)	0	A. Palmer (halved)	0
K. Bousfield	0	W. Casper (5 and 3)	1
D. J. Rees (2 and 1)	1	J. Hebert	0
N. C. Coles (halved)	0	G. Littler (halved)	0
B. J. Hunt (5 and 4)	1	J. Barber	0
C. O'Connor	0	D. Finsterwald (2 and 1)	1

Afternoon

	Matches		Matches
H. Weetman	0	A. Wall (1 hole)	1
P. Alliss (3 and 2)	1	W. Collins	0
B. J. Hunt	0	M. Souchak (2 and 1)	1
T. B. Haliburton	0	A. Palmer (2 and 1)	1
D. J. Rees (4 and 3)	1	D. Ford	0
K. Bousfield (1 hole)	1	J. Barber	0
N. C. Coles (1 hole)	1	D. Finsterwald	0
C. O'Connor (halved)	0	G. Littler (halved)	0
	—		—
	6	(three halved)	7

Grand Aggregates: Great Britain, 8 matches; U.S.A., 13 matches, with 3 matches halved.
Captains: D. J. Rees, Great Britain, and Jerry Barber, U.S.A.

At Atlanta, Georgia, October 11th, 12th and 13th, 1963.

FOURSOMES
Morning

U.S.A.	Matches	GREAT BRITAIN	Matches
A. Palmer and J. Pott	0	B. G. C. Huggett and G. Will (3 and 2)	1
W. Casper and D. Ragan (1 hole)	1	P. Alliss and C. O'Connor	0
J. Boros and A. Lema (halved)	0	N. C. Coles and B. J. Hunt (halved)	0
G. Littler and D. Finsterwald (halved)	0	D. C. Thomas and H. Weetman (halved)	0

Afternoon

	Matches		Matches
W. Maxwell and R. Goalby (4 and 3)	1	D. C. Thomas and H. Weetman	0
A. Palmer and W. Casper (5 and 4)	1	B. G. C. Huggett and G. Will	0
G. Littler and D. Finsterwald (2 and 1)	1	N. C. Coles and G. M. Hunt	0
J. Boros and A. Lema (1 hole)	1	T. B. Haliburton and B. J. Hunt	0
	—		—
	5		1

Totals: U.S.A., 5; Great Britain, 1 (two halved)

FOUR BALL
Morning

U.S.A.	Matches	GREAT BRITAIN	Matches
A. Palmer and D. Finsterwald (5 and 4)	1	B. G. C. Huggett and D. C. Thomas	0
G. Littler and J. Boros (halved)	0	P. Alliss and B. J. Hunt (halved)	0

W. Casper and W. Maxwell (3 and 2)	1	H. Weetman and G. Will	0
R. Goalby and D. Ragan	0	N. C. Coles and C. O'Connor (1 hole)	1
	2		1

Afternoon

A. Palmer and D. Finsterwald (3 and 2)	1	N. C. Coles and C. O'Connor	0
A. Lema and J. Pott (1 hole)	1	P. Alliss and B. J. Hunt	0
W. Casper and W. Maxwell (2 and 1)	1	T. B. Haliburton and G. M. Hunt	0
R. Goalby and D. Ragan (halved)	0	B. G. C. Huggett and D. C. Thomas (halved)	0
	3		0

Totals: U.S.A., 5 Great Britain 1 (two halved)

SINGLES
Morning

U.S.A.	Matches	GREAT BRITAIN	Matches
A. Lema (5 and 3)	1	G. M. Hunt	0
J. Pott	0	B. G. C. Huggett (3 and 1)	1
A. Palmer	0	P. Alliss	1
W. Casper (halved)	0	N. C. Coles (halved)	0
R. Goalby (3 and 2)	1	D. C. Thomas	0
G. Littler (1 hole)	1	C. O'Connor	0
J. Boros	0	H. Weetman (1 hole)	1
D. Finsterwald	0	B. J. Hunt (2 holes)	1
	3		4

Afternoon

U.S.A.	Matches	GREAT BRITAIN	Matches
A. Palmer (3 and 2)	1	G. Will	0
D. Ragan (2 and 1)	1	N. C. Coles	0
A. Lema (halved)	0	P. Alliss (halved)	0
G. Littler (6 and 5)	1	T. B. Haliburton	0
J. Boros (2 and 1)	1	H. Weetman	0
W. Maxwell (2 and 1)	1	C. O'Connor	0
D. Finsterwald (4 and 3)	1	D. C. Thomas	0
R. Goalby (2 and 1)	1	B. J. Hunt	0
	7		0

Totals: U.S.A., 10; Great Britain, 4 (two halved).
Grand Aggregates: U.S.A., 20; Great Britain, 6 (six halved)
Captains: A. Palmer, U.S.A.; J. Fallon (non-playing), Great Britain.

At Royal Birkdale, October 7th, 8th and 9th, 1965

FOURSOMES
Morning

GREAT BRITAIN	Matches	U.S.A.	Matches
D. C. Thomas and G. Will (6 and 5)	1	D. Marr and A. Palmer	0
C. O'Connor and P. Alliss (5 and 4)	1	K. Venturi and D. January	0
L. Platts and P. J. Butler	0	J. Boros and A. Lema (1 hole)	1
B. J. Hunt and N. C. Coles	0	W. Casper and G. Littler (2 and 1)	1

Afternoon

D. C. Thomas and G. Will	0	D. Marr and A. Palmer (6 and 5)	1
J. Martin and J. Hitchcock	0	J. Boros and A. Lema (5 and 4)	1
C. O'Connor and P. Alliss (2 and 1)	1	W. Casper and G. Littler	0
B. J. Hunt and N. C. Coles (3 and 2)	1	K. Venturi and D. January	0
	4		4

Totals: Great Britain, 4; U.S.A., 4.

FOUR-BALL
Morning

GREAT BRITAIN	Matches	U.S.A.	Matches
D. C. Thomas and G. Will	0	D. January and T. Jacobs (1 hole)	1
L. Platts and P. J. Butler (halved)	0	W. Casper and G. Littler (halved)	0
P. Alliss and C. O'Connor	0	D. Marr and A. Palmer (5 and 4)	1
N. C. Coles and B. J. Hunt (1 hole)	1	J. Boros and A. Lema	0

Afternoon

P. Alliss and C. O'Connor (1 hole)	1	D. Marr and A. Palmer	0
D. C. Thomas and G. Will	0	D. January and T. Jacobs (1 hole)	1
L. Platts and P. J. Butler (halved)	0	W. Casper and G. Littler (halved)	0
N. C. Coles and B. J. Hunt	0	A. Lema and K. Venturi (1 hole)	1
	2		4

Totals: Great Britain, 6; U.S.A., 8 (with 2 halved).

SINGLES
Morning

GREAT BRITAIN	Matches	U.S.A.	Matches
J. Hitchcock	0	A. Palmer (3 and 2)	1
L. Platts	0	J. Boros (4 and 2)	1
P. J. Butler	0	A. Lema (1 hole)	1
N. C. Coles	0	D. Marr (2 holes)	1
B. J. Hunt (2 holes)	1	G. Littler	0
P. Alliss (1 hole)	1	W. Casper	0
D. C. Thomas	0	T. Jacobs (2 and 1)	1
G. Will (halved)	0	D. January (halved)	0

Afternoon

P. J. Butler	0	A. Palmer (2 holes)	1
J. Hitchcock	0	J. Boros (2 and 1)	1
C. O'Connor	0	A. Lema (6 and 4)	1
P. Alliss (3 and 1)	1	K. Venturi	0
B. J. Hunt	0	D. Marr (1 hole)	1
N. C. Coles (3 and 2)	1	W. Casper	0
G. Will	0	G. Littler (2 and 1)	1
L. Platts (1 hole)	1	T. Jacobs	0
	5		10

Grand Aggregates: Great Britain, 11; U.S.A., 18 (with 3 halved).
Non-playing Captains: H. Weetman, Great Britain; Byron Nelson, U.S.A.

At Houston, Texas, October 20th, 21st and 22nd, 1967.

FOURSOMES
Morning

U.S.A.	Matches	GREAT BRITAIN	Matches
W. Casper and J. Boros (halved)	0	B. G. C. Huggett and G. Will (halved)	0
A. Palmer and G. Dickinson (2 and 1)	1	P. Alliss and C. O'Connor	0
D. Sanders and G. Brewer	0	A. Jacklin and D. C. Thomas (4 and 3)	1
B. Nichols and J. Pott (6 and 5)	1	B. J. Hunt and N. C. Coles	0

Afternoon

J. Boros and W. Casper (1 hole)	1	B. G. C. Huggett and G. Will	0
G. Dickinson and A. Palmer (5 and 4)	1	M. Gregson and H. F. Boyle	0
G. Littler and A. Geiberger	0	A. Jacklin and D. C. Thomas (3 and 2)	1
B. Nichols and J. Pott (2 and 1)	1	P. Alliss and C. O'Connor	0
	5		2

Totals: U.S.A., 5; Great Britain 2 (1 halved).

FOUR-BALL
Morning

U.S.A.	Matches	GREAT BRITAIN	Matches
W. Casper and G. Brewer (3 and 2)	1	P. Alliss and C. O'Connor	0
B. Nichols and J. Pott (1 hole)	1	B. J. Hunt and N. C. Coles	0
G. Littler and A. Geiberger (1 hole)	1	A. Jacklin and D. C. Thomas	0
G. Dickinson and D. Sanders (3 and 2)	1	B. G. C. Huggett and G. Will	0

Afternoon

W. Casper and G. Brewer (5 and 3)	1	B. J. Hunt and N. C. Coles	0
G. Dickinson and D. Sanders (3 and 2)	1	P. Alliss and M. Gregson	0
A. Palmer and J. Boros (1 hole)	1	G. Will and H. F. Boyle	0
G. Littler and A. Geiberger (halved)	0	A. Jacklin and D. C. Thomas (halved)	0
	7		0

Totals: U.S.A., 12; Great Britain 2 (2 halved).

SINGLES
Morning

U.S.A.	Matches	GREAT BRITAIN	Matches
G. Brewer (4 and 3)	1	H. F. Boyle	0
W. Casper (2 and 1)	1	P. Alliss	0
A. Palmer (3 and 2)	1	A. Jacklin	0
J. Boros	0	B. G. C. Huggett (1 hole)	1
D. Sanders	0	N. C. Coles (2 and 1)	1
A. Geiberger (4 and 2)	1	M. Gregson	0
G. Littler (halved)	0	D. C. Thomas (halved)	0
B. Nichols (halved)	0	B. J. Hunt (halved)	0

157

Afternoon

A. Palmer (5 and 3)	1	B. G. C. Huggett	0
G. Brewer	0	P. Alliss (2 and 1)	1
G. Dickinson (3 and 2)	1	A. Jacklin	0
B. Nichols (3 and 2)	1	C. O'Connor	0
J. Potts (3 and 1)	1	G. Will	0
A. Geiberger (2 and 1)	1	M. Gregson	0
J. Boros (halved)	0	B. J. Hunt (halved)	0
D. Sanders	0	N. C. Coles (2 and 1)	1
	9		4

Grand Aggregates: U.S.A., 21; Great Britain, 6 (with 5 halved).
Non-playing Captains: B. Hogan, U.S.A.; D. J. Rees, Great Britain.

At Royal Birkdale, September 18th, 19th and 20th, 1969.

FOURSOMES
Morning

GREAT BRITAIN		U.S.A.	
	Matches		*Matches*
N. C. Coles, B. G. C. Huggett (3 and 2)	1	M. Barber and R. Floyd	0
B. Gallacher, M. Bembridge (2 and 1)	1	L. Trevino and K. Still	0
A. Jacklin and P. Townsend (3 and 1)	1	D. Hill and T. Aaron	0
C. O'Connor and P. Alliss (halved)	0	W. Casper and F. Beard (halved)	0

Afternoon

N. C. Coles, B. G. C. Huggett	0	D. Hill and T. Aaron (1 hole)	1
B. Gallacher and M. Bembridge	0	L. Trevino and G. Littler (2 holes)	1
A. Jacklin and P. Townsend (1 hole)	1	W. Casper and F. Beard	0
B. J. Hunt and P. J. Butler	0	J. Nicklaus and D. Sikes (1 hole)	1
	4		3

Foursomes Totals: Great Britain 4; U.S.A. 3 (1 halved).

FOUR-BALL
Morning

C. O'Connor and P. Townsend (1 hole)	1	D. Hill and D. Douglass	0
B. G. C. Huggett, G. A. Caygill (halved)	0	R. Floyd and M. Barber (halved)	0
B. Barnes and P. Alliss	0	L. Trevino and G. Littler (1 hole)	1
A. Jacklin and N. C. Coles (1 hole)	1	J. Nicklaus and D. Sikes	0

Afternoon

P. Townsend and P. J. Butler	0	W. Casper and F. Beard (2 holes)	1
B. G. C. Huggett, B. Gallacher	0	D. Hill and K. Still (2 and 1)	1
M. Bembridge and B. J. Hunt (halved)	0	T. Aaron and R. Floyd (halved)	0
A. Jacklin and N. C. Coles (halved)	0	L. Trevino and M. Barber (halved)	0
	2		3

Four-Ball Totals: Great Britain 2; U.S.A. 3 (3 halved).

SINGLES
Morning

P. Alliss	0	L. Trevino (2 and 1)	1
P. Townsend	0	D. Hill (5 and 4)	1
N. C. Coles (1 hole)	1	T. Aaron	0
B. Barnes	0	W. Casper (1 hole)	1
C. O'Connor (5 and 4)	1	F. Beard	0
M. Bembridge (1 hole)	1	K. Still	0
P. J. Butler (1 hole)	1	R. Floyd	0
A. Jacklin (4 and 3)	1	J. Nicklaus	0

Afternoon

B. Barnes	0	D. Hill (4 and 2)	1
B. Gallacher (4 and 3)	1	L. Trevino	0
M. Bembridge	0	M. Barber (7 and 6)	1
P. J. Butler (3 and 2)	1	D. Douglass	0
C. O'Connor	0	G. Littler (2 and 1)	1
B. G. C. Huggett (halved)	0	W. Casper (halved)	0
N. C. Coles	0	D. Sikes (4 and 3)	1
A. Jacklin (halved)	0	J. Nicklaus (halved)	0
	7		7

Singles Totals: Great Britain 7; U.S.A. 7 (2 halved).
Grand Aggregates: Great Britain 13; U.S.A. 13 (6 halved).
Non-playing captains: E. C. Brown, Great Britain; S. Snead, U.S.A.

At St. Louis, Missouri, September 16th, 17th and 18th, 1971

FOURSOMES
Morning

U.S.A.		GREAT BRITAIN	
	Matches		*Matches*
W. J. Casper and M. Barber	0	N. C. Coles and C. O'Connor (2 and 1)	1
A. Palmer and G. Dickinson (2 holes)	1	P. M. P. Townsend and P. A. Oosterhuis	0
J. W. Nicklaus and D. Stockton	0	B. G. C. Huggett and A. Jacklin (3 and 2)	1
C. Coody and F. Beard	0	M. E. Bembridge and P. J. Butler (1 hole)	1

Afternoon

W. J. Casper and M. Barber	0	H. Bannerman and B. J. Gallacher (2 and 1)	1
A. Palmer and G. Dickinson (1 hole)	1	P. M. P. Townsend and P. A. Oosterhuis	0
L. Trevino and M. Rudolph (halved)	0	B. G. C. Huggett and A. Jacklin (halved)	0
J. W. Nicklaus and J. C. Snead (5 and 3)	1	M. E. Bembridge and P. J. Butler	0
	3		4

Foursomes Totals: U.S.A. 3; Great Britain 4 (1 halved).

FOUR-BALL
Morning

L. Trevino and M. Rudolph (2 and 1)	1	C. O'Connor and B. W. Barnes	0
F. Beard and J. C. Snead (2 and 1)	1	N. C. Coles and J. Garner	0
A. Palmer and G. Dickinson (5 and 4)	1	P. A. Oosterhuis and B. J. Gallacher	0
J. W. Nicklaus and G. Littler (2 and 1)	1	P. M. P. Townsend and H. Bannerman	0

Afternoon

L. Trevino and W. J. Casper	0	B. J. Gallacher and P. A. Oosterhuis (1 hole)	1
G. Littler and J. C. Snead (2 and 1)	1	A. Jacklin and B. G. C. Huggett	0
A. Palmer and J. W. Nicklaus (1 hole)	1	P. M. P. Townsend and H. Bannerman	0
C. Coody and F. Beard (halved)	0	N. C. Coles and C. O'Connor (halved)	0
	6		1

Four-Ball Totals: U.S.A. 6; Great Britain 1; (1 halved).

SINGLES
Morning

L. Trevino (1 hole)	1	A. Jacklin	0
D. Stockton (halved)	0	B. J. Gallacher (halved)	0
M. Rudolph	0	B. W. Barnes (1 hole)	1
G. Littler	0	P. A. Oosterhuis (4 and 3)	1
J. W. Nicklaus (3 and 2)	1	P. M. P. Townsend	0
G. Dickinson (5 and 4)	1	C. O'Connor	0
A. Palmer (halved)	0	H. Bannerman (halved)	0
F. Beard (halved)	0	N. C. Coles (halved)	0

Afternoon

L. Trevino (7 and 6)	1	B. G. C. Huggett	0
J. C. Snead (1 hole)	1	A. Jacklin	0
M. Barber	0	B. W. Barnes (2 and 1)	1
D. Stockton (1 hole)	1	P. M. P. Townsend	0
C. Coody	0	B. J. Gallacher (2 and 1)	1
J. W. Nicklaus (5 and 3)	1	N. C. Coles	0
A. Palmer	0	P. A. Oosterhuis (3 and 2)	1
G. Dickinson	0	H. Bannerman (2 and 1)	1
	7		6

Singles Totals: U.S.A. 7; Great Britain 6 (3 halved).
Grand Aggregates: U.S.A. 16; British Isles 11 (5 halved).
Non-Playing Captains: Jay Hebert, U.S.A.; E.C. Brown, Great Britain.

At Muirfield, September 20th, 21st and 22nd, 1973

FIRST DAY – FOURSOMES

GREAT BRITAIN AND IRELAND		U.S.A.	
	Matches		*Matches*
B. W. Barnes and B. J. Gallacher (1 hole)	1	L. Trevino and W. J. Casper	0
C. O'Connor and N. C. Coles (3 and 2)	1	T. Weiskopf and J. C. Snead	0
A. Jacklin and P. A. Oosterhuis (halved)	0	J. Rodriguez and L. Graham (halved)	0
M. E. Bembridge and E. Polland	0	J. W. Nicklaus and A. Palmer (6 and 5)	1
	4		1

FOUR-BALLS

GREAT BRITAIN AND IRELAND		U.S.A.	
	Matches		*Matches*
B. W. Barnes and B. J. Gallacher (5 and 4)	1	T. Aaron and G. Brewer	0
M. E. Bembridge and B. G. C. Huggett (3 and 1)	1	A. Palmer and J. W. Nicklaus	0
A. Jacklin and P. A. Oosterhuis (3 and 1)	1	T. Weiskopf and W. J. Casper	0
C. O'Connor and N. C. Coles	0	L. Trevino and H. Blancas (2 and 1)	1
	3		1

First Day Totals: Great Britain and Ireland 5; U.S.A., 2 (1 halved).

SECOND DAY – FOURSOMES

B. W. Barnes and P. J. Butler	0	J. W. Nicklaus and T. Weiskopf (1 hole)	1
P. A. Oosterhuis and A. Jacklin (2 holes)	1	A. Palmer and D. Hill	0
M. E. Bembridge and B. G. C. Huggett (5 and 4)	1	J. Rodriguez and L. Graham	0
N. C. Coles and C. O'Connor	0	L. Trevino and W. J. Casper (2 and 1)	1

FOUR-BALLS

B. W. Barnes and P. J. Butler	0	J. C. Snead and A. Palmer (2 holes)	1
A. Jacklin and P. Oosterhuis	0	G. Brewer and W. J. Casper (3 and 2)	1
C. Clark and E. Polland	0	J. W. Nicklaus and T. Weiskopf (3 and 2)	1
M. E. Bembridge and B. G. C. Huggett (halved)	0	L. Trevino and H. Blancas (halved)	0
	2		5

Second Day Totals: Great Britain and Ireland, 2; U.S.A., 5 (1 halved).

THIRD DAY SINGLES

Morning

B. W. Barnes	0	W. J. Casper (2 and 1)	1
B. J. Gallacher	0	T. Weiskopf (3 and 1)	1
P. J. Butler	0	H. Blancas (5 and 4)	1
A. Jacklin (3 and 1)	1	T. Aaron	0
N. C. Coles (halved)	0	G. Brewer (halved)	0
C. O'Connor	0	J. C. Snead (1 hole)	1
M. E. Bembridge (halved)	0	J. W. Nicklaus (halved)	0
P. A. Oosterhuis (halved)	0	L. Trevino (halved)	0

Afternoon

B. G. C. Huggett (4 and 2)	1	H. Blancas	0
B. W. Barnes	0	J. C. Snead (3 and 1)	1
B. J. Gallacher	0	G. Brewer (6 and 5)	1
A. Jacklin	0	W. J. Casper (2 and 1)	1
N. C. Coles	0	L. Trevino (6 and 5)	1
C. O'Connor (halved)	0	T. Weiskopf (halved)	0
M. E. Bembridge	0	J. W. Nicklaus (2 holes)	1
P. A. Oosterhuis (4 and 2)	1	A. Palmer	0
	3		9

Singles Totals: Great Britain and Ireland, 3; U.S.A., 9 (4 halved).
Grand Aggregates: Great Britain and Ireland, 10; U.S.A., 16 (6 halved).
Non-playing Captains: B. J. Hunt, Great Britain and Ireland; J. Burke, U.S.A.

At Laurel Valley, Pennsylvania, September 19th, 20th and 21st, 1975.

FIRST DAY – FOURSOMES

U.S.A.		GREAT BRITAIN AND IRELAND	
	Matches		*Matches*
J. W. Nicklaus and T. Weiskopf (5 and 4)	1	B. W. Barnes and B. J. Gallacher	0
G. Littler and H. Irwin (4 and 3)	1	N. Wood and M. Bembridge	0
A. Geiberger and J. Miller (3 and 1)	1	A. Jacklin and P. Oosterhuis	0
L. Trevino and J. C. Snead (2 and 1)	1	T. Horton and J. O'Leary	0
	4		0

FOUR-BALLS

W. J. Casper and R. Floyd	0	P. Oosterhuis and A. Jacklin (2 and 1)	1
T. Weiskopf and L. Graham (3 and 2)	1	E. Darcy and C. O'Connor, Jun	0
J. W. Nicklaus and R. Murphy (halved)	0	B. W. Barnes and B. J. Gallacher (halved)	0
L. Trevino and H. Irwin (2 and 1)	1	T. Horton and J. O'Leary	0
	2		1

First Day Totals: U.S.A. 6; Great Britain and Ireland 1 (1 halved).

SECOND DAY – FOUR-BALLS

W. J. Casper and J. Miller (halved)	0	P. Oosterhuis and A. Jacklin (halved)	0
J. W. Nicklaus and J. C. Snead (4 and 2)	1	T. Horton and N. Wood	0
G. Littler and L. Graham (5 and 3)	1	B. W. Barnes and B. J. Gallacher	0
A. Geiberger and R. Floyd (halved)	0	E. Darcy and G. L. Hunt (halved)	0
	2		0

FOURSOMES

L. Trevino and R. Murphy	0	A. Jacklin and B. W. Barnes (3 and 2)	1
T. Weiskopf and J. Miller (5 and 3)	1	C. O'Connor and J. O'Leary	0
H. Irwin and W. J. Casper (3 and 2)	1	P. Oosterhuis and M. Bembridge	0
A. Geiberger and L. Graham (3 and 2)	1	E. Darcy and G. L. Hunt	0
	3		1

Second Day Totals: U.S.A. 5; Great Britain and Ireland 1 (2 halved).

THIRD DAY SINGLES

Morning

R. Murphy (2 and 1)	1	A. Jacklin	0
J. Miller	0	P. Oosterhuis (2 holes)	1
L. Trevino (halved)	0	B. J. Gallacher (halved)	0
H. Irwin (halved)	0	T. Horton (halved)	0
G. Littler (4 and 2)	1	B. G. C. Huggett	0
W. J. Casper (3 and 2)	1	E. Darcy	0
T. Weiskopf (5 and 3)	1	G. L. Hunt	0
J. W. Nicklaus	0	B. W. Barnes (4 and 2)	1

Afternoon

R. Floyd (1 hole)	1	A. Jacklin	0
J. C. Snead	0	P. Oosterhuis (3 and 2)	1
A. Geiberger (halved)	0	B. J. Gallacher (halved)	0
L. Graham	0	T. Horton (2 and 1)	1
H. Irwin (2 and 1)	1	J. O'Leary	0
R. Murphy (2 and 1)	1	M. Bembridge	0
L. Trevino	0	N. Wood (2 and 1)	1
J. W. Nicklaus	0	B. W. Barnes (2 and 1)	1
	7		6

Third Day Totals: U.S.A., 7; Great Britain and Ireland 6 (3 halved).
Grand Aggregates: U.S.A. 18; Great Britain and Ireland 8 (6 halved).
Non-playing Captains: A. Palmer, U.S.A.; B. J. Hunt, Great Britain

At Royal Lytham and St. Annes, September 15th, 16th and 17th, 1977

FIRST DAY – FOURSOMES

GREAT BRITAIN AND IRELAND		U.S.A.	
	Matches		*Matches*
B. J. Gallacher and B. W. Barnes	0	L. Wadkins and H. Irwin (3 and 1)	1
N. C. Coles and M. James	0	D. Stockton and J. McGee (1 hole)	1
N. Faldo and P. Oosterhuis (2 and 1)	1	R. Floyd and L. Graham	0
E. Darcy and A. Jacklin (halved)	0	E. Sneed and D. January (halved)	0
T. Horton and M. James	0	J. W. Nicklaus and T. Watson (5 and 4)	1
	1		3

SECOND DAY – FOUR-BALLS

B. W. Barnes and T. Horton	0	T. Watson and H. Green (5 and 4)	1
N. C. Coles and P. Dawson	0	E. Sneed and L. Wadkins (5 and 3)	1
N. Faldo and P. Oosterhuis (3 and 1)	1	J. W. Nicklaus and R. Floyd	0
A. Jacklin and E. Darcy	0	D. Hill and D. Stockton (5 and 3)	1
M. James and K. Brown	0	H. Irwin and L. Graham (1 hole)	1
	1		4

THIRD DAY – SINGLES

H. Clark	0	L. Wadkins (4 and 3)	1
N. C. Coles	0	L. Graham (5 and 3)	1
P. Dawson (5 and 4)	1	D. January	0
B. W. Barnes (1 hole)	1	H. Irwin	0
T. Horton	0	D. Hill (5 and 4)	1
B. J. Gallacher (1 hole)	1	J. W. Nicklaus	0
E. Darcy	0	H. Green (1 hole)	1
M. James	0	k. Floyd (2 and 1)	1
N. Faldo (1 hole)	1	T. Watson	0
P. Oosterhuis (2 holes)	1	J. McGee	0
	5		5

Match Aggregate: Great Britain and Ireland 7: U.S.A. 12 (1 halved).
Non-playing Captains: B. G. C. Huggett, Great Britain and Ireland; D. Finsterwald, U.S.A.

At Greenbrier, West Virginia, September 14th, 15th and 16th, 1979

FIRST DAY – FOUR-BALLS

U.S.A.	Matches	GREAT BRITAIN AND EUROPE	Matches
L. Wadkins and L. Nelson (2 and 1)	1	A. Garrido and S. Ballesteros	0
L. Trevino and F. Zoeller (3 and 2)	1	K. Brown and M. James	0
A. Bean and L. Elder (2 and 1)	1	P. Oosterhuis and N. Faldo	0
H. Irwin and J. Mahaffey	0	B. Gallacher and B. Barnes (2 and 1)	1
	3		1

FOURSOMES

H. Irwin and T. Kite (7 and 6)	1	K. Brown and D. Smyth	0
F. Zoeller and H. Green	0	S. Ballesteros and A. Garrido (3 and 2)	1
L. Trevino and G. Morgan (halved)	0	A. Lyle and T. Jacklin (halved)	0
L. Wadkins and L. Nelson (4 and 3)	1	B. Gallacher and B. Barnes	0
	2		1

SECOND DAY – FOURSOMES

L. Elder and J. Mahaffey	0	T. Jacklin and A. Lyle (5 and 4)	1
A. Bean and T. Kite	0	N. Faldo and P. Oosterhuis (6 and 5)	1
F. Zoeller and M. Hayes	0	B. Gallacher and B. Barnes (2 and 1)	1
L. Wadkins and L. Nelson (3 and 2)	1	S. Ballesteros and A. Garrido	0
	1		3

FOUR-BALLS

L. Wadkins and L. Nelson (5 and 4)	1	S. Ballesteros and A. Garrido	0
H. Irwin and T. Kite (1 hole)	1	T. Jacklin and A. Lyle	0
L. Trevino and F. Zoeller	0	B. Gallacher and B. Barnes (3 and 2)	1
L. Elder and M. Hayes	0	N. Faldo and P. Oosterhuis (1 hole)	1
	2		2

THIRD DAY – SINGLES

L. Wadkins	0	B. Gallacher (3 and 2)	1
L. Nelson (3 and 2)	1	S. Ballesteros	0
T. Kite (1 hole)	1	T. Jacklin	0
M. Hayes (1 hole)	1	A. Garrido	0
A. Bean (4 and 3)	1	M. King	0
J. Mahaffey (1 hole)	1	B. Barnes	0
L. Elder	0	N. Faldo (3 and 2)	1
H. Irwin (5 and 3)	1	D. Smyth	0
H. Green (2 holes)	1	P. Oosterhuis	0
F. Zoeller	0	K. Brown (1 hole)	1
L. Trevino (2 and 1)	1	A. Lyle	0
G. Morgan (halved, match not played)	0	M. James (halved, match not played, injured)	0
	8		3

Match Aggregate: U.S.A. 16; Great Britain and Europe 10 (2 halved).
Non-playing Captains: W. Casper, U.S.A.; J. Jacobs, Great Britain and Europe.

At Walton Heath, September 18th to 20th, 1981

FOURSOMES

EUROPE	Matches	U.S.A.	Matches
B. Langer and M. Pinero	0	L. Trevino and L. Nelson (1 hole)	1
A. Lyle and M. James (2 and 1)	1	W. Rogers and B. Lietzke	0
B. Gallacher and D. Smythe (3 and 2)	1	H. Irwin and R. Floyd	0
P. Oosterhuis and N. Faldo	0	T. Watson and J. Nicklaus (4 and 3)	1
	2		2

FOURBALLS
Afternoon

S. Torrance and H. Clark (halved)	0	T. Kite and J. Miller (halved)	0
A. Lyle and M. James (3 and 2)	1	B. Crenshaw and J. Pate	0
D. Smythe and J-M. Canizares (6 and 5)	1	W. Rogers and B. Lietzke	0
B. Gallacher and E. Darcy	0	H. Irwin and R. Floyd (2 and 1)	1
	2		1

FOURBALLS
Morning

N. Faldo and S. Torrance	0	L. Trevino and J. Pate (7 and 5)	1
A. Lyle and M. James	0	L. Nelson and T. Kite (1 hole)	1
B. Langer and M. Pinero (2 and 1)	1	R. Floyd and H. Irwin	0
J-M. Canizares and D. Smyth	0	J. Nicklaus and T. Watson (3 and 2)	1
	1		3

FOURSOMES
Afternoon

P. Oosterhuis and S. Torrance	0	L. Trevino and J. Pate (2 and 1)	1
B. Langer and M. Pinero	0	J. Nicklaus and T. Watson (3 and 2)	1
A. Lyle and M. James	0	W. Rogers and R. Floyd (3 and 2)	1
D. Smyth and B. Gallacher	0	T. Kite and L. Nelson (3 and 2)	1
	0		4

SINGLES

S. Torrance	0	L. Trevino (5 and 3)	1
A. Lyle	0	T. Kite (3 and 2)	1
B. Gallacher (halved)	0	W. Rogers (halved)	0
M. James	0	L. Nelson (2 holes)	1
D. Smyth	0	B. Crenshaw (6 and 4)	1
B. Langer (halved)	0	B. Lietzke (halved)	0
M. Pinero (4 and 2)	1	J. Pate	0
J-M. Canizares	0	H. Irwin (1 hole)	1
N. Faldo (2 and 1)	1	J. Miller	0
H. Clark (4 and 3)	1	T. Watson	0
P. Oosterhuis	0	R. Floyd (1 hole)	1
E. Darcy	0	J. Nicklaus (5 and 3)	1
	3		7

Grand Aggregate: Europe, 8; U.S.A, 17 (3 halved)
Captains: J. Jacobs, Europe, and D. Marr, U.S.A.

PGA National, Florida, October 14th-16th, 1983

FOURSOMES
Morning

U.S.A.	Matches	EUROPE	Matches
T. Watson and B. Crenshaw (5 and 4)	1	B. J. Gallacher and A. Lyle	0
L. Wadkins and C. Stadler	0	N. Faldo and B. Langer (4 and 2)	1
R. Floyd and B. Gilder	0	J-M. Canizares and S. Torrance (4 and 3)	1
T. Kite and C. Peete (2 and 1)	1	S. Ballesteros and P. Way	0
	2		2

FOURBALLS
Afternoon

G. Morgan and F. Zoeller	0	B. Waites and K. Brown (2 and 1)	1
T. Watson and J. Haas (2 and 1)	1	N. Faldo and B. Langer	0
R. Floyd and C. Strange	0	S. Ballesteros and P. Way (1 hole)	1
B. Crenshaw and C. Peete (halved)	0	S. Torrance and I. Woosnam (halved)	0
	1		2

FOURBALLS
Morning

C. Stadler and L. Watkins (1 hole)	1	B. Waites and K. Brown	0
C. Peete and B. Crenshaw	0	N. Faldo and B. Langer (4 and 2)	1
G. Morgan and J. Haas (halved)	0	S. Ballesteros and P. Way (halved)	0
T. Watson and B. Gilder (5 and 4)	1	S. Torrance and I. Woosnam	0
	2		1

FOURSOMES
Afternoon

T. Kite and R. Floyd	0	N. Faldo and B. Langer (3 and 2)	1
L. Wadkins and G. Morgan (7 and 5)	1	S. Torrance and J-M. Canizares	0
T. Watson and B. Gilder	0	S. Ballesteros and P. Way (2 and 1)	1
J. Haas and C. Strange (3 and 2)	1	B. Waites and K. Brown	0
	2		2

SINGLES

F. Zoeller (halved)	0	S. Ballesteros (halved)	0
J. Haas	0	N. Faldo (2 and 1)	1
G. Morgan	0	B. Langer (2 holes)	1
B. Gilder (2 holes)	1	G. Brand, Snr	0
B. Crenshaw (3 and 1)	1	A. Lyle	0
C. Peete (1 hole)	1	B. Waites	0
C. Strange	0	P. Way (2 and 1)	1
T. Kite (halved)	0	S. Torrance (halved)	0
C. Stadler (3 and 2)	1	I. Woosnam	0
L. Wadkins (halved)	0	J-M. Canizares (halved)	0
R. Floyd	0	K. Brown (4 and 3)	1
T. Watson (2 and 1)	1	B. Gallacher	0
	5		4

Grand Aggregate: USA, 12; Europe, 11 (5 halved).
Captains: A. Jacklin, Europe, J. W. Nicklaus, U.S.A.